WITHDRAWN

American Indian and Eskimo Authors

American Indian and Eskimo Authors

a comprehensive bibliography

Compiled by Arlene B. Hirschfelder

Association on American Indian Affairs: New York

The Association on American Indian Affairs (432 Park Avenue South, New York, N. Y. 10016) is a private, non-profit, national citizens' organization supported by members and contributions. It assists Indian and Alaska Native communities in their efforts to achieve full economic, social, and civil equality.

The Association also has published *American Indian Authors for Young Readers: A Selected Bibliography,* compiled and with an introduction by Mary Gloyne Byler. It is available from Interbook Inc., 545 Eighth Avenue, New York, N.Y. 10018. $1.00.

Z
1209
H55

Copyright © 1973 Association on American Indian Affairs

Library of Congress Catalog Card Number 73-82109

Printed in the United States of America

Distributed by Interbook Inc.

Cover: John S. Timber, author of *Cheyenne Memories,* photographed by Martin J. Dain

Foreword

Compiled to inform the general public of the large body of Native American literature, this is the most comprehensive bibliography of American Indian and Eskimo authors ever published. It is a revised and greatly enlarged edition of a bibliography published by the Association on American Indian Affairs in 1970. It contains almost 400 titles written or narrated by nearly 300 Indian and Eskimo authors representing more than 100 tribes—more than twice as extensive as the first edition. We hope this encourages readers to learn firsthand about historical and contemporary Native affairs.

The literary contributions of American Indians and Eskimos often have gone unnoticed because of the peculiar way publishers and bibliographers have listed books authored by them. It has long been customary to promote books under the names of the investigators or editors who record or revise material written or narrated by Natives rather than under the names of the people who deserve the primary credit—the Indians and Eskimos themselves. All works in this bibliography are listed under the names of the Indians or Eskimos who narrated or wrote them.

Because of the current interest in Native culture and history, many of the books listed in this bibliography as "out of print" may well become available from reprint houses such as AMS Press, Johnson Reprint Corporation, and Kraus Reprint Company. It would be worthwhile to inquire of these presses whether they have reprinted books authored by Indians and Eskimos since the publication of this bibliography.

In addition to works cited in this bibliography, readers who are interested in firsthand written accounts by Natives should consult series such as:

> American Anthropologist
> American Antiquarian
> Anthropological Papers of the American Museum of Natural History
> Columbia University Contributions to Anthropology
> Field Columbian Museum Anthropological Series
> General Series in Anthropology
> Journal of American Folklore
> Memoirs of the American Anthropological Association
> Memoirs of the American Folklore Society
> Memoirs of the American Museum of Natural History
> Proceedings of the American Antiquarian Society
> Publications of the American Ethnological Society
> Publications of the Carnegie Institute of Washington
> Publications of the Field Columbian Museum
> Smithsonian Contributions to Anthropology
> U. S. Bureau of American Ethnology, Annual Reports and Bulletins
> University of California Publications in American Archaeology
>   and Ethnology
> University of Pennsylvania Museum Anthropology Publications
> University of Washington Publications in Anthropology

Other firsthand accounts by Indians and Eskimos may be found in manuscript collections and Canadian and European libraries.

Arlene B. Hirschfelder

Preface

Down through the years, American Indians have had to struggle to survive in this, their homeland. The struggle still goes on. Mere physical existence is but one aspect of this struggle. Cultural survival—the preservation of traditional institutions, religions, values, lifeways—is equally important. This insistence on surviving as Indians has made the struggle more, not less, difficult.

At the turn of the century, fifty-five thousand acres of land which the Indian people of Taos Pueblo regard as their church were seized by the federal government for inclusion in a national forest. In the 1920s the Taos religious leaders were jailed by federal authorities for practicing their religion. Not so long ago Northern Cheyenne members of the Native American Church were arrested for worshipping the Creator. Generations of Indian children have been forbidden to speak their language at school and their parents can remember the day when the government severely punished them for performing their tribal ceremonies.

Today the people of Taos Pueblo have had their sacred lands restored to them. The Native American Church is freed from government interference. Indian children are learning in their schools about their own history and culture and, in a few cases, are being taught in their Native languages. The federal government is encouraging foreign tourists to visit the reservations and observe tribal ceremonies. These changes do not reflect new attitudes of American Indians; instead they indicate a moderation in non-Indian attitudes—a growing respect.

Public attitudes have, and have had, profound and usually tragic implications for American Indian tribes. Publishers, authors, motion picture and television producers, journalists and teachers must bear a fair measure of responsibility. Perhaps recent improvements in Indian and white relations can be attributed to the fact that the public now is beginning to recognize that it is time to listen to the Indians themselves—to learn from them about their insights into the human condition and about their hopes, not only for themselves but for all mankind.

This is not to say that the grave problems facing American Indian communities are rapidly disappearing. Indian unemployment today stands at nearly 50%. The average age at death is 46. Approximately 25% of all Indian children are taken from their families, often without cause and without due process of law, and placed in non-Indian foster homes, adoptive homes, and institutions.

The American public has learned and has still much to learn from American Indians. American Indians are unique on this continent. Their beliefs, values, religions and insights are different from any brought here by peoples from other lands. American Indian thought is exciting and at times profound, it is wise, humorous, and imaginative. Surely Black Elk, the Sioux holy man, has something very moving and important to say to all Americans. To read him is to learn something about ourselves.

It is not the purpose of this bibliography to idealize American Indian authors. Books by American Indians can be as slanted, self-serving, inaccurate, or as foolish as books by anyone else. Its purpose is to present American Indians *as they are,* through their writings, for all their human faults and for all their magnificence. Here are American Indians speaking for themselves, unmediated by non-Indians.

Being Indian—from whatever tribe—is more than an intellectual exercise, an emotional choice, or discovery of an Indian ancestor in the family tree. Being Indian is growing up Indian. It is a way of being, a way of life. Non-Indians, shaped by their own experience, perceive the world around them through their particular cultural and historical adjustment to life. A vast body of literature about American Indians by non-Indian authors has grown up presenting a broad range of stereotypes about American Indians—ranging from the "noble savage" to the bloodthirsty warrior. These stereotypes have been manipulated by non-Indians to fulfill some illusory public or personal need. We shall not be a mature nation until we can stop and listen to what American Indians have said about our past—and what they are saying today about the quality of our life and condition of our society.

Mary Gloyne Byler
Member, Eastern Band of Cherokee Indians of North Carolina

Tribal Index

ABENAKI
Oledoska

ACOMA PUEBLO
Anonymous
Paytiamo, James (Flaming Arrow)

APACHE
Betzinez, Jason
Geronimo
Hoffman, Joseph
Kaywaykla, James
Kenoi, Samuel E.
Maria, Casa
Mockingbird, Jon
Pesita, Juan
Prince, Anna
Valor, Palmer

ARAPAHO
Anonymous
Sweezy, Carl

ASSINIBOINE
Dumont, Robert V., Jr.
Kennedy, Dan (Ochankugahe)
Long, James Larpenteur
   (First Boy)

ATHABASCAN
Huntington, James

BELLA BELLA
Gladstone, Willy

BLACKFEET
Bad Head
Tatsey, John
Welch, James

CAHUILLA
Chief Meyers
Costo, Rupert
Patencio, Chief Francisco
Saubel, Katherine Siva

CARRIER
Erickson, Sheila

CATAWBA
Brown, Margaret Wiley
Gordon, Sally
Owl, Mrs. Samson

CHEROKEE
Adair, William P.
Ax, John
Beeler, Joe
Black Fox (Inâ'li, Ino:li)
Boudinot, Elias
Boudinot, Elias Cornelius
Bronson, Ruth Muscrat
Brown, Catherine
Brown, Margaret Wiley
Fry, Maggie Culver
Gahuni
Gordon, Sally
Kilpatrick, Anna Gritts
Kilpatrick, Jack Frederick
Momaday, Natachee Scott
Oskison, John Milton
Owens, Narcissa
Owl, Mrs. Samson
Ridge, John Rollin (Yellow Bird)
Ridge, Major
Ross, John
Russell, Norman H.
Sanders, Thomas (Nippawanock)
Swimmer
Thomas, Robert K.

CHEROKEE *(Continued)*
Traveller Bird (Tsisghwanai)
Wafford, James D.
Wahnenauhi (Lucy Lowry Hoyt Keys)
Watie, Stand

CHEYENNE
Anonymous
Cohoe, William
Henson, Lance
Howling Wolf
Stands in Timber, John
Tall Bull, Henry
Wooden Leg

CHINOOK
Cultee, Charles

CHIPPEWA
Antell, Will
Copway, George
  (Kah-Ge-Ga-Gah-Bowh)
En-me-gah-bowh
Grisdale, Alex
Jacobs, Peter (Pah-tah-se-ga)
Johnston, Patronella
Jones, Rev. Peter
  (Kah-Ke-Wa-Quo-Na-By)
King, Cheryl Mills
  (Wah-be-gwo-nese)
Laduke, Vincent (Sun Bear)
Maungwudaus
Morriseau, Norval
Redbird, Duke
Redsky, James
  (Esquekesik)
Rogers, John
  (Chief Snow Cloud)
Thompson, Chief Albert Edward
Vaudrin, Bill
Vizenor, Gerald
Warren, William Whipple
Waubageshig (Harvey McCue)

CHOCTAW
Folsom, Israel
Folsom-Dickerson, W. E. S.
Garland, Samuel
Pitchlynn, Peter Perkins
Tubbee, Okah
Wright, Muriel Hazel

CLACKAMAS CHINOOK
Howard, Victoria

COLVILLE
Pierre, Chief George

COOS
Buchanan, Jim

CREE
Boulanger, Tom
Cardinal, Harold
Ray, Carl
Sainte-Marie, Buffy
Wuttunee, William I. C.

CREEK
Posey, Alexander Lawrence
Tchikilli

CROATAN
Long Lance, Chief Buffalo Child

CROW
Plenty-Coups
Plenty Hawk
Pretty Shield
Two Leggings
Yellow Brow
Young Crane

DELAWARE
Anonymous
Calvin, Hezekiah

ESKIMO
  Anauta
  Anonymous
  Attungoruk
  Barr, Martha
  Comock
  Markoosie
  Mayokok, Robert
  Nuligak
  Okakok
  Oquilluk, William
  Pitseolak
  Romer, Herman
  Senungetuk, Joseph
  Stalker, Marie
  Willoya, William

FLATHEAD
  McNickle, D'Arcy

FOX
  Anonymous

GROS VENTRE
  Blackbird
  Jones, Bill
  Watches-All

HAIDA
  Isaac
  McGregor, Walter
  Reid, William
  Stevens, Tom

HIDATSA
  Goodbird, Edward

HOPI
  Bahnimptewa, Cliff
  Crow-Wing
  Fredericks, Oswald White Bear
  Kabotie, Fred
  Katchongva, Dan
  Nequatewa, Edmund
  Qoyawayma, Polingaysi
    (Elizabeth Q. White)

HOPI *(Continued)*
  Sekaquaptewa, Emory
  Sekaquaptewa, Helen
  Talayesva, Don C.

ISLETA PUEBLO
  Lorenso

JEMEZ PUEBLO
  Sando, Joe S.

KALAPUYA
  Hudson, John B.

KASHAYA
  Antone, David
  James, Herman
  Parrish, Essie

KIOWA
  Kickingbird, Kirke
  Momaday, N. Scott
  Zo-Tom

KIOWA-APACHE
  Whitewolf, Jim

KLALLAM
  Niatum, Duane

KLIKITAT
  Hunt, Joe

KWAKIUTL
  Anonymous
  Nowell, Charles James
  Sewid, James

LOUCHEAUX
  Josie, Edith

LUISENO
  Hyde, Villiana

MAIDU
  Young, Tom

MENOMINEE
  Satterlee, Captain John Valentine
  Satterlee, Joseph
  Satterlee, Josephine

MICMAC
  Brooks, Benjamin

MINSI
  Bedford, Denton R.

MODOC
  Riddle, Jeff

MOHAWK
  Anonymous
  Deserontyou, John
  Fadden, Ray (Aren Akweks)
  Johnson, E. Pauline
    (Tekahionwake)
  Monture, Ethel Brant
  Newell, William B.

MOHAWK-DELAWARE
  Lone Dog, Louise

MOHEGAN
  Ashpo, Samuel
  Fielding, Fidelia A. H.
  Occom, Samson

NARRAGANSETT-WAMPANOAG
  Peek, William (Metacomet)

NATCHEZ
  Stiggins, George

NAVAJO
  Begay, Beyal
  Bennett, Kay
  Bighorse, Tiana
  Cha-la-pí

NAVAJO *(Continued)*
  Curly, River Junction
  Curly, Slim
  Johnson, Jay Ralph
  Klah, Hasteen
  Left Handed
  Mitchell, Emerson Blackhorse
  Mitchell, Frank
  Morgan, William
  Mr. Moustache
  Old Man Buffalo Grass
  Old Mexican
  Singer Man
  Son of Former Many Beads
  Yazzie, Ethelon
  Yuinth-Zezi

NEVADA INDIANS
  Anonymous

NEZ PERCE
  Armstrong, Chief Ralph
  Chief Joseph
  Nez Perce Tribe
  Phinney, Archie
  Yellow Wolf

NOOTKA
  Clutesi, George C.
  George, Hamilton
  Tom
  Williams, Frank

ODAWA
  Pelletier, Wilfred

OKANOGAN
  Hum-ishu-ma (Mourning Dove)

OMAHA
  LaFlesche, Francis
  Wolf Killer(?)

ONEIDA
  Dockstader, Frederick J.

OSAGE
  Griffis, Joseph K.
    (Chief Tahan)
  Kimball, Yeffe
  Mathews, John Joseph

OTOMI
  Villaseñor, David

OTTAWA
  Blackbird, Chief Andrew J.
    (Mack-e-te-be-nessy)

PAIUTE
  Hopkins, Sarah Winnemucca
  Lowry, Annie
  Newland, Sam
  Stewart, Jack
  Tillohash, Tony

PAPAGO
  Chona, Maria

PASSAMAQUODDY
  Josephs, Noel
  Josephs, Tomah

PAWNEE
  Murie, James R.

PENOBSCOT
  Lion, Newell
  Mitchell, Wayne
  Neptune, Martin
  Neptune, Noel
  Nicolar, Joseph
  Thompson, Jean

PEQUOT
  Apes, William

PICURIS PUEBLO
  Vargas, Rosendo

PIMA
  Shaw, Anna Moore
  Webb, George

POMO
  Allen, Elsie
  Benson, W. Ralganal
  Benson, William
  Coon, Bill
  James, Bill
  Pot, Bob

PONCA
  Black Eagle

POTAWATOMI
  Pokagon, Chief Simon

POWHATAN
  Forbes, Jack D.

SAN JUAN PUEBLO
  Ortiz, Alfonso

SANTA CLARA PUEBLO
  Dozier, Edward P.
  Velarde, Pablita

SAUK
  Black Hawk

SAUK and FOX
  Young Bear, Ray

SENECA
  Cornplanter, Jessie L.
  Farmer's Brother
  Gabourie, Fred Whitedeer
  Parker, Arthur Caswell
  Parker, Chief Everett
  Pierce, Chief Maris Bryant
  Red Jacket
  Strong, Nathaniel

SENECA-CAYUGA
Winnie, Lucile "Jerry"
(Sah-gan-de-oh)

SHAWNEE
Alford, Thomas Wildcat

SHINNECOCK
Hunter, Lois Marie

SHOSHONE
Stump, Sarain

SHUSWAP
Manuel, George

SIOUX
Anonymous
Bad Heart Bull, Amos
Big Eagle, Jerome
(Wambde-tonka)
Black Elk
Burnette, Robert
Chief Eagle, Dallas
Deloria, Ella Cara
Deloria, Vine, Jr.
Deloria, Vine V., Sr.
Ducheneaux, Karen
Eastman, Charles Alexander
Flying Cloud, Chief
(Francis Benjamin Zahn)
Flying Hawk
Lame Deer, Chief John (Fire)
LaPointe, Frank
LaPointe, James
McGaa, Ed
McLaughlin, Marie L.
Red Horse Owner
Sitting Bull
Sneve, Virginia Driving Hawk
Standing Bear, Luther
White Bull, Joseph
Yellow Robe, Rosebud
(Lacotawin)
Zitkala-Sä (Gertrude Bonnin)

SLAVEY
Tetso, John

SOUTHERN DIEGUENO
Cuero, Delphina

SPOKANE
Wynecoop, David C.

TAKELMA
Johnson, Frances

TAOS PUEBLO
Concha, Joseph L.

TEWA
See San Juan Pueblo and
Santa Clara Pueblo

TLINGET
Cameron, Don
Dekinā′k![u]
Katishan

TSIMSHIAN
Tate, Henry W.

TUSCARORA
Cusick, David
Hewitt, John Napoleon Brinton
Johnson, Chief Elias
Rickard, Chief Clinton

UTE
Mack, Charlie

WAILAKI
Young, Lucy

WALAPAI
Blind Tom
Kuni
Paul

WAWENOOK
 Neptune, Francois

WINNEBAGO
 Anonymous
 Crashing Thunder
 Mountain Wolf Woman

WINTU
 Towendolly, Grant

WISHRAM
 McGuff, Pete
 Simpson, Louis
 Simpson, Tom

WYANDOTT
 Clarke, Peter Dooyentate

YANA
 Bat'wi, Sam
 Brown, Betty

YAQUI
 Castro, Ambrosio A.
 Chavez, Lucas
 Lopez, Rafael
 Moisés, Rosalio

ZUNI PUEBLO
 Anonymous
 Clarence
 Peynetsa, Andrew
 Sanchez, Walter
 Zuni, Flora
 Zuni, Linda
 Zuni Pueblo

MISCELLANEOUS
 American Indian Historical Society
 Amerind Club, University of Arizona
 Conference on California Indian Education
 Indian Children of British Columbia
 Indians of All Tribes
 Institute of American Indian Arts Students
 Iroquois League of Nations
 National Indian Brotherhood
 Porcupine Day School Students
 Shishmaref Day School Students
 Taos Pueblo Day School Students
 Working Indians Civil Association

American Indian and Eskimo Authors

ADAIR, WILLIAM P., Cherokee, see BOUDINOT, ELIAS CORNELIUS.

ALFORD, THOMAS WILDCAT, Shawnee
Civilization, as told to Florence Drake. Norman: Univ. of Oklahoma Press, 1936. 203 pp. Illus. Out of print.

The author, a great-grandson of Tecumseh, discusses Shawnee life and history and his own schooling and work in Shawnee affairs.

ALLEN, ELSIE, Pomo
Pomo Basketmaking: A Supreme Art for the Weaver. Healdsburg, California: Naturegraph Publishers, 1972. 67 pp. Illus. $5.00. Also paperbound: $2.00.

An autobiography of Elsie Allen, born in 1899 in California, who is the fourth generation of Pomo basket weavers, accompanies detailed descriptions and accurate drawings and photographs (some illustrating the fingers of Elsie Allen doing each step in the process) of how to make baskets.

AMERICAN INDIAN HISTORICAL SOCIETY
The American Indian Reader. Book One: Anthropology; Book Two: Education; Book Three: Literature; Book Four: History; and Book Five: Current Affairs. San Francisco: Indian Historian Press. Each book: $3.00 paperbound. The complete set of five: $12.50.

These five books contain information on Native American history, culture, literature and current affairs. Each book covers its specific subject with the best articles from *The Indian Historian,* together with new articles prepared for the series.

Indian Voices: The First Convocation of American Indian Scholars. San Francisco: The Indian Historian Press, 1970. $9.00 paperbound.†

Native American scholars from across the Nation met in 1970 at Princeton University. This book contains the formal presentations that were made and the uninhibited discussions that followed. Religion, art, literature, education, civil rights, history, tribal government, the urban scene and tribal economy were discussed.

Indian Voices: The Second Convocation: Native Americans Today. San Francisco: The Indian Historian Press. $7.00 paperbound.†

The second convocation of American Indian scholars was held at the Aspen Institute for Humanistic Studies, Colorado. This book contains the open discussion of contemporary problems facing Indians: health and medicine, communications, water and land rights, education today, and curriculum development. Suggested solutions are included.

Textbooks and the American Indian. San Francisco: The Indian Historian Press, 1970. 269 pp. $4.25.

The study evaluates the treatment of American Indians in 160 textbooks now in use in both the public schools and the Bureau of Indian Affairs schools in the United States. A list of criteria for evaluating material is included.

AMERIND CLUB, University of Arizona
Indians and 1976: Native Americans Look at the American Revolution Bicentennial Observance, ed. by Joy Chaudhuri. Tucson: Univ. of Arizona, 1973. 66 pp. $1.25 paperbound. Available from: Amerind Club, Univ. of Arizona, Tucson, Arizona 85721.

---

*The Indian Historian Press is a private publishing venture organized by members of the American Indian Historical Society. Its purpose is to publish books by Indians about the history, culture, and current condition of American Indians.

The Press has many titles scheduled for publication. To secure information on new titles write: The Indian Historian Press, 1451 Masonic Ave., San Francisco, Calif. 94117.

†Two volumes, *First* and *Second Convocations:* $14.00.

This booklet contains, in summary form, the speeches, resolutions, recommendations and discussions presented during the American Indian Week Conference at the University of Arizona in January of 1973. The material represents an exchange of Indian views regarding the coming bicentennial celebration of the American Revolution.

ANAUTA, Eskimo
Children of the Blizzard, with Heluiz Chandler Washburne. London: Dennis Dobson, 1960. 192 pp. Illus. 75 shillings (about $4.00). Can be ordered through British Book Center, Inc., 996 Lexington Ave., New York, N. Y. 10027.

The author uses her own experiences as background for a series of interrelated stories about several Baffin Island Eskimo children. Different types of work—hunting, securing food, constructing shelter, making clothes—are described, as are friendships, relationships between adults and children, games and travel. A concluding chapter on games shows that they are not just for fun but are important for survival. A vocabulary of Eskimo words is included.

Land of the Good Shadows: The Life Story of Anauta, an Eskimo Woman, with Heluiz Chandler Washburne. New York: John Day Co., 1940. 329 pp. Illus. Out of print.

This life story of a Baffin Island Eskimo woman, recorded when she was approximately 45 years old, covers her marriage, death of her husband and contacts with white society. The last chapter is a critical essay on white civilization. An Eskimo alphabet and glossary are included.

Wild Like the Foxes: The True Story of an Eskimo Girl. New York: John Daly, 1956. 192 pp. Out of print.

This story is based on the life of the author's mother, Alea, and covers her girlhood up until she meets Yorgke who becomes her husband. Hunting, trapping, playing boys' games, enduring hardships are all part of Alea's life until she is sent to school in England by her widowed father. Her return to Labrador, her love for Yorgke, and the death of her father are described.

ANONYMOUS, Acoma Pueblo
Autobiography of an Acoma Indian, ed. by Leslie A. White, U. S. Bureau of American Ethnology, Bulletin 136, Anthropological Papers No. 32. Washington: Government Printing Office, 1943. pp. 326-337. Out of print.

An autobiographical sketch given by a 73-year-old Acoma man in 1941 reveals Acoma history and daily life. The informant's story illustrates the career of a Pueblo culture subjected to inroads of American culture.

ANONYMOUS, Arapaho
"Narrative of an Arapaho Woman," ed. by Truman Michelson. *American Indian Anthropologist,* No. 35. Menasha, Wisc.: American Anthropological Association, 1933. pp. 565-610. Out of print.

This narrative of a 72-year-old woman, given through an interpreter, reveals the culture of the Arapaho Tribe as well as the role of a woman in Arapaho society during the last half of the nineteenth century.

ANONYMOUS, Cheyenne
Narrative of a Southern Cheyenne Woman, ed. by Truman Michelson. Smithsonian Miscellaneous Collections, Vol. 87, No. 5. Washington: Smithsonian Institution, 1932. 13 pp. Out of print.

A Cheyenne woman of the late nineteenth and early twentieth centuries describes her marriage and family life and tribal customs, beliefs, ceremonies, games, etc.

ANONYMOUS, Delaware
"The Walam Olum, or Red Score, of the Lenâpé," in Daniel G. Brinton: *The Lenâpé and Their Legends; With the Complete Text and Symbols of the Walam Olum.* New York: AMS Press, Inc. pp. 170-232. $8.00.

An essay discussing the origin, authenticity and contents of the Walam Olum precedes the manuscript of pictographic symbols which illustrate ancient Delaware tribal traditions and gives an historical record of Delaware migrations in North America. The symbols have both a Delaware and English explanation. This is a reprint of a book published in 1885 by Daniel Brinton as Volume 5 in his Library of Aboriginal American Literature.

ANONYMOUS, Eskimo
Anerca, ed. by Edmound Carpenter. Toronto: J. M. Dent, Ltd., 1972. Unpaged. Illus. $4.50. Also paperbound: $2.50.

Poems and songs from Eskimo groups living across the tundra and taiga of Alaska and Canada to the icebound coast of East Greenland are presented with illustrations by Enooesweetok of Baffin Island that were collected by Robert Flaherty in 1913-14.

I Breathe a New Song: Poems of the Eskimo, ed. by Richard Lewis. New York: Simon and Schuster, Inc., 1971. 128 pp. Illus. $5.95.

Ninety representative Eskimo poems in this collection include magical chants, lullabies, songs to bring luck while hunting, and songs to taunt enemies. An introduction by Lewis describes Eskimo people, their beliefs, and ways of forming poetry.

Tales from the Igloo, ed. by Father Maurice Metayer. Edmonton, Alberta: Hurtig Publishers, 1972. 128 pp. Illus. $4.95.

This is a collection of 22 legends of the Copper Eskimo people who inhabit the Canadian Arctic coast. Adventures of Eskimo children and intrigues of animal characters reveal the life style of Eskimos as well as the Eskimo view of men, women, nature and the supernatural.

ANONYMOUS, Fox

The Autobiography of a Fox Woman, ed. by Truman Michelson. U. S. Bureau of American Ethnology, Fortieth Annual Report. Washington: Government Printing Office, 1925. pp. 291-349. Out of print.

The narrative life story of a Fox woman (whose name is withheld on agreement) is presented in Fox and English texts. The narrator discusses her life during the late nineteenth and early twentieth centuries and the customs and beliefs of the Fox Tribe at that time.

ANONYMOUS, Kwakiutl

Kwakiutl Tales, ed. by Franz Boas. Part I: Translations; Part II: Texts. New York: AMS Press, Inc. $34.00. Part Part, $18.00.

Kwakiutl tales narrated by several members of the tribe are presented in Kwakiutl and English texts (British Columbia). This is a reprint of Columbia Univ. Contributions to Anthropology, Vol. XXVI, 1935-1943.

ANONYMOUS, Mohawk

The Iroquois Book of Rites, ed. by Horatio Hale. New York: AMS Press, Inc. 222 pp. $8.00.

Ancient ceremonies, speeches, and songs (from two manuscripts recited by Chief John "Smoke" Johnson and interpreted by his son Chief George H. M. Johnson, both Mohawks) provide a picture of Iroquois political and social life in the Northeast. This is a reprint of a book published in 1883 by Daniel Brinton as Volume 2 in his Library of Aboriginal American Literature.

ANONYMOUS, Nevada Indians

Nevada Indians Speak, ed. by Jack D. Forbes. Reno: Univ. of Nevada Press, 1967. 293 pp. Illus. Out of print.

This collection of first-person statements deals with first encounters with white men and the struggle to maintain an identity despite the influx of a new and dominant culture.

ANONYMOUS, Sioux

The Hardin Winter Count, ed. by David Finster. Museum News, Vol. 26, Nos. 3-4. March-April, 1968. Vermillion, South Dakota: Univ. of South Dakota, 1968. 59 pp. Illus. Out of print.

This winter count,* collected from an unknown member of the Rosebud Sioux Tribe sometime between 1895 and 1902, records events for each winter from 1776-1879. Information on the Sioux Tribe and its relations with other tribes is provided. Interpretations and comments on each pictograph, drawn from Indian and non-Indian sources, are included.

ANONYMOUS, Winnebago

"Personal Reminiscences of a Winnebago Indian," ed. by Paul Radin, in *The Journal of American Folklore,* Vol. 26, 1913. pp. 293-318. New York: Kraus Reprint Co. $18.00 paperbound.

A Winnebago man, approximately 48 years old, relates a version of a favorite story among his tribe and reminisces about his childhood and eventual involvement with the medicine dance ceremony. Winnebago and English texts are included.

ANONYMOUS, Zuni Pueblo

Zuni Origin Myths, ed. by Ruth L. Bunzel, U. S. Bureau of American Ethnology, Forty-Seventh Annual Report. Washington: Government Printing Office, 1932. pp. 545-609. Out of print.

The Zuni origin myth is presented both in its esoteric ritual form, as used for religious instruction, and in its informal, narrative form. In addition, there is a ritual account of the origin of the masked dancing of the Katchina society.

Zuni Ritual Poetry, ed. by Ruth L. Bunzel. U. S. Bureau of American Ethnology, Forty-Seventh Annual Report. Washington: Government Printing Office, 1932, pp. 611-835. Out of print.

---

*Winter count: A picture of the main event each winter. Because the Plains Indians traveled far on their long hunts and met people from other tribes, they made wider use of pictographs than did Indians of other regions. Pictographs were also used for messages, warnings, and treaties, as well as histories.

Ritual poetry of Zunis, preceded by an essay about the nature and function of prayer, includes prayers to the Ancients, sun, and Uwanammi; prayers of the war and medicine cults; and prayers and chants of the priests of the masked gods.

ANTELL, WILL, Chippewa
William Warren. Minneapolis: Dillon Press, 1973. 56 pp. Illus. $4.95.

This biography of William Whipple Warren, who was born in 1825, includes information on his family, work in the Territorial House of Representatives of which he was the only Indian member, his articles for a newspaper in St. Paul and his writing of a book about the Chippewas. Also included are Chippewa legends and customs as well as information about fur trading.

ANTONE, DAVID, Kashaya, see JAMES, HERMAN.

APES, WILLIAM, Pequot
A Son of the Forest: The Experience of William Apes, A Native of the Forest. New York: Published by the Author, 1831. 214 pp. Out of print.

In the first part of the book Apes, born in 1798 in Massachusetts, describes his childhood sufferings, the different people who raised, owned or hired him, his life in the army, and the strong influence Christianity had on his life, which eventually led him to become a preacher. The second part of the book contains an appendix of numerous "general observations" regarding Indians by which Apes tries to represent the Natives' true character.

Eulogy on King Philip: As Pronounced at the Odeon. Boston: Published by the Author, 1836. 60 pp. Out of print.

Apes' eulogy to Philip, a Wampanoag Indian, includes a history of Native-white relations from the first contact, Philip's relationships with colonists during the 1660's and 1670's and the events leading up to "King Philip's War." The eulogy can also be read as an attack on bigotry and intolerance.

Indian Nullification of the Unconstitutional Laws of Massachusetts Relative to the Marchpee Tribe; or The Pretended Riot Explained. Boston: Press of Jonathan Howe, 1835. 168 pp. Out of print.

The book describes the events by which Apes, an ordained minister who has gone among the Marshpee to preach, gets involved in their affairs which results in his being convicted and imprisoned for helping members of the tribe prevent a white man from carrying wood off Marshpee land. Apes' work in trying to rid the tribe of unjust state laws is also described.

ARMSTRONG, CHIEF RALPH, Nez Perce
"Some Nez Perce Traditions Told by Chief Armstrong," ed. by Ella E. Clark. *Oregon Historical Quarterly,* Vol. LIII, No. 3, Sept. 1952. pp. 181-191. Out of print.

Chief Armstrong, born in 1871 in Oregon, relates in English many of the traditions of the Nez Perce he learned from his grandmother and grandfather.

ASHPO, SAMUEL, and **OCCOM, SAMSON,** Mohegan; **CALVIN, HEZEKIAH,** Delaware, *et al.*
The Letters of Eleazar Wheelock's Indians, ed. by James Dow McCallum. Dartmouth Manuscript Series, No. 1. Hanover, New Hampshire: Dartmouth College Publication, 1932. 327 pp. Illus. $5.00. Available from Archives Department, Baker Memorial Library, Dartmouth College, Hanover, N. H. 03755.

Indians attending Moor's Charity School, founded by Eleazar Wheelock in Connecticut and eventually located in New Hampshire, reveal their feelings and experiences in letters written to Wheelock while they attended the school from 1754-79. An appendix lists the names of all the Indians who attended the school during that period.

ATTUNGORUK, Eskimo
"The Autobiography of an Alaskan Eskimo," ed. by James W. VanStone, *Arctic,* Vol. 10, No. 4, pp. 195-210. Out of print.

Attungoruk, a Point Hope Eskimo born in 1928, covers events in his life from childhood through his first jobs and travels in Fairbanks and Anchorage to his return to Point Hope. The autobiography illustrates the problems arising from being taught a moral code irrelevant to the Eskimo cultural tradition.

AX, JOHN, Cherokee, see SWIMMER; AX, JOHN; WAFFORD, JAMES D., *et al.,* Cherokee.

BAD HEAD, Blackfeet
A Blackfoot Winter Count, ed. by Hugh A. Dempsey. Calgary, Alberta: Glenbow Foundation, 1965. 20 pp. $.75 paperbound. Available from Museum Sales Desk, Glenbow-Alberta Institute, 901 11th Avenue, S.W., Calgary 3, Alberta, Canada.

Bad Head's winter count is a calendrical and historical record of the years 1810-1883. It provides information on the Blackfeet Tribe and its relations with other tribes. Literal translations for each Blackfeet term and comments on each count, drawn from a number of sources, are included.

BAD HEART BULL, AMOS, Sioux

A Pictographic History of the Oglala Sioux, text by Helen H. Blish. Lincoln: Univ. of Nebraska Press, 1967. 562 pp. Illus. by author. $17.95.

Over four-hundred drawings and notations done by Bad Heart Bull between 1890 and 1913 are incorporated in this volume to provide a visual record of Sioux culture. The text provides background, identities and interpretation of the symbols.

BAHNIMPTEWA, CLIFF, Hopi

Dancing Kachinas. Phoenix, Arizona: Heard Museum of Anthropology and Primitive Art, 1971. 34 pp. Illus. $2.00 paperbound. Available from: Heard Museum, 22 E. Monte Vista, Phoenix, Ariz. 85004.

This collection of paintings by a Hopi artist depicts in color kachinas from all three mesas, reflecting many phases of Hopi religion and portraying the kachina society as living beings.

BARR, MARTHA; ROMER, HERMAN, STALKER, MARIE, *et al.,* Eskimo

Tales of Eskimo Alaska, ed. by O. W. Frost. Anchorage, Alaska: Alaska Methodist University Press, 1971. 91 pp. Illus. $4.50. Also paperbound: $2.50.

This collection of 21 legends and stories is divided into four sections: Togiak Tales for Children, Bethel Tales for Children, Legends of the lower Yukon and Kuskokwim and Legends of Kotzebue and vicinity. All informants are cited in the "Contents."

BAT'WĪ, SAM, and BROWN, BETTY, Yana

Yana Texts, collected by Edward Sapir. New York: Kraus Reprint Co., 1964. pp. 1-235. $25.00 paperbound.

A collection of myths obtained in 1907 in California represent the Northern Yana and Central Yana dialects. Both Yana and English texts are provided. A supplementary section of Yana myths collected by Dr. R. B. Dixon from Sam Bat'wi and Round Mountain Jack is included. This is a reprint of Univ. of California Publications in American Archaeology and Ethnology, Vol. 9, No. 1, 1910-1911.

BEDFORD, DENTON R., Minsi

Tsali. San Francisco: The Indian Historian Press, 1972. 252 pp. Illus. $9.00.

The author writes an historic novel about Tsali, a Cherokee man, who survived the Georgia Army bandits in 1838, the year of the infamous Cherokee removal, who loved the earth and all its creatures, and defended the Cherokee religious faith and ancient Cherokee traditions.

BEELER, JOE, Cherokee

Cowboys and Indians: Characters in Oil and Bronze. Norman: Univ. of Oklahoma Press, 1967. 167 pp. Illus. by author. $7.95.

Reproductions of Beeler's paintings, drawings, and bronzes are accompanied by his explanations of the works.

BEGAY, BEYAL, Navajo

Astsah or Eagle Catching Myth, retold in shorter form by Mary C. Wheelwright. Bulletin No. 3. Santa Fe, New Mexico: Museum of Navajo Ceremonial Art, Inc., 1949. pp. 1-10. $.50 paperbound and $.15 postage. Available from Museum of Navajo Ceremonial Art, P. O. Box 5153, Santa Fe, N. M. 87501.

The adventures of Nayenezgani (Man of the First Earth), who had a spirit wind to counsel him, are described in this booklet.

BENNETT, KAY, Navajo

Kaibah: Recollections of a Navajo Girlhood. Los Angeles: Western Lore Press, 1964. 253 pp. Illus. by author. $7.50.

This autobiographical story of a Navajo girl and her family takes place in New Mexico and covers the years from 1928 to 1935. Each chapter presents a vignette of Navajo life as experienced by the author in her childhood.

A Navajo Saga, with Russ Bennett. San Antonio, Texas: The Naylor Company, 1969. 239 pp. Illus. $6.95.

The author presents a family history covering the period of 1846-1870 in New Mexico. It is a time during which Navajos are hunted down, forced into submission, marched on foot to Bosque Redondo, where they suffer hardships for four years until the treaty of 1868 permits them to return to their homeland.

BENSON, W. RALGANAL, Pomo
"Pomo Creation Myth," ed. by J. de Angulo, in *The Journal of American Folklore*, Vol. 48, No. 189, 1935. pp. 203-262. New York: Kraus Reprint Co. $18.00 paperbound.

The Pomo story of creation is accompanied by a literal rendering in English closely following Pomo idioms and style (California).

BENSON, WILLIAM, Pomo
"The Stone and Kelsey 'Massacre' on the Shores of Clear Lake in 1849: the Indian Viewpoint." *California Historical Society Quarterly*, Vol. XI, No. 3, Sept., 1932. pp. 266-273. Out of print.

Benson gives an account of the 1849 slaying of two white men in California, basing his description on information gathered from tribal members. His account is not only an historical document, it also provides an insight into Indian psychology in Indian-white relations.

BETZINEZ, JASON, Apache
I Fought with Geronimo, with Wilbur S. Nye. Harrisburg, Pennsylvania: Stackpole Books, 1959. 214 pp. Illus. Out of print.

This book was written in English by Betzinez when he was nearly 100 years old. In it, he presents a military history describing his Apache group's intermittent warfare against Anglos, Mexicans and other Indians, including information about the leadership and tactics of Geronimo and other Apaches.

BIG EAGLE, JEROME (WAMBDE-TONKA), Sioux
"A Sioux Story of the War." *Minnesota Historical Society Collections,* Vol. 6, Part 3, 1894. pp. 382-400. Out of print.

Mr. Big Eagle narrates through an interpreter his story of the Sioux war in Minnesota in 1862, from the outbreak to surrender, explaining why and how the Sioux fought and the causes of the war, with comments on the campaigns and battles.

BIGHORSE, TIANA, Navajo
Working with the Wool: How to Weave a Navajo Rug, co-authored by Noel Bennett. Flagstaff, Arizona: Northland Press, 1971. 103 pp. Illus. $4.95 paperbound.

This resource book on the Navajo approach to weaving is a first step in making Navajo techniques available to any interested person. Chapters cover equipment needed, warping the loom, weaving basics, design considerations, and what to do when things go wrong.

BLACK EAGLE, Ponca
"Xube, a Ponca Autobiography," ed. by William Whitman, in *The Journal of American Folklore,* Vol. 52, 1939. pp. 180-193. New York: Kraus Reprint Co. $18.00 paperbound.

This narrative of Black Eagle, a Ponca born in 1889 in Oklahoma, who possessed a limited amount of "xube" (supernatural) power, covers his early experiences with the supernormal and the supernatural.

BLACK ELK, Sioux
Black Elk Speaks: Being the Life Story of a Holy Man of the Oglala Sioux, as told to John G. Neihardt. Lincoln: Univ. of Nebraska Press, 1961. 281 pp. Illus. by Standing Bear. $1.50 paperbound.

Originally published in 1932, this is a personal narrative by one of the great spiritual leaders of the Oglala Sioux. Black Elk, a holy man who was born in 1863, gives a moving account of his life from early boyhood to the massacre at Wounded Knee in 1890 and the gathering of the Oglala Sioux on the Pine Ridge Reservation in South Dakota.

The Sacred Pipe: Black Elk's Account of the Seven Rites of the Oglala Sioux, ed. by Joseph Epes Brown. Norman: Univ. of Oklahoma Press, 1953. 144 pp. Illus. $5.95. Also paperbound: Baltimore: Penguin Books, Inc., $1.45.

Narrated by Black Elk when he was over 90 years of age, this is an account of sacred Sioux religious ceremonies.

BLACK HAWK, Sauk
Black Hawk: An Autobiography, ed. by Donald Jackson. Gloucester, Massachusetts: Peter Smith, 1955. 206 pp. Illus. $4.00. Also paperbound: Urbana: Univ. of Illinois Press, $1.75.

In this autobiography, based on an 1833 version, Black Hawk narrates to a government interpreter a seventy-year struggle from his early battles with other tribes to his last flight from the United States Army.

BLACKBIRD, Gros Ventre, see JONES, BILL.

BLACKBIRD, CHIEF ANDREW J. (MACK-E-TE-BE-NESSY), Ottawa

History of the Ottawa and Chippewa Indians of Michigan; A Grammar of Theirr Language, and Personal and Family History of the Author. Ypsilanti, Michigan: Ypsilantian Job Printing House, 1887. 128 pp. Out of print.

Blackbird provides a history of the Ottawa Tribe, and incidentally of the Chippewa Tribe, including names of leaders, what tribes the Ottawa contended with before and after arriving in Michigan, and how the Tribe came to be settled in Michigan. Also included are legends, Blackbird's own personal and family histories, and translations of the Ottawa and Chippewa grammars into English.

BLIND TOM, Walapai, see KUNI.

BOUDINOT, ELIAS, Cherokee

An Address to the Whites. Philadelphia: William F. Geddes, 1826. 16 pp. Out of print.

In this speech delivered on May 26, 1826, Boudinot gives a general and informative discussion about his tribe, indicating its progress and deploring the possible extinction of his or any other Indian tribe.

BOUDINOT, ELIAS CORNELIUS, Cherokee

Remarks of Elias C. Boudinot of the Cherokee Nation on Behalf of the Bill to Organize the Territory of Oklahoma. Washington, D.C.: M'Gill and Witherow, 1874. 18 pp. Out of print.

Boudinot's remarks before the House Committee on Territories are a reply to points made in an argument by Colonel W. P. Ross, who represents the Cherokee delegation opposed to the bill to organize the Territory of Oklahoma.

Speech of Elias C. Boudinot, a Cherokee Indian, On The Indian Question, Delivered at Vinita, Cherokee Nation, September 21, 1871. Washington: M'Gill and Witherow, 1872. 18 pp. Out of print.

In a speech he gives in support of Congress passing a bill to organize the territory of Oklahoma out of Indian Territory, Boudinot advocates abolishment of the tribal land system in favor of lands owned in severalty. He also advocates the establishment of U. S. courts in Indian Territory and sees advantages to be derived by securing representation in Congress.

Speech of Elias C. Boudinot, of the Cherokee Nation, Delivered at Vinita, Indian Territory, August 29, 1874. St. Louis: Barns and Beynon, 1874. 40 pp. Out of print.

In this speech, Boudinot tries to show that the tribal land system is unreliable and subject to extinguishment at any time without consent, and that tribal governments are extravagant and corrupt. He urges abolishment of the tribal land system and adoption of lands owned in severalty. He also discusses his differences with William P. Ross, a Cherokee with opposing views.

BOUDINOT, ELIAS CORNELIUS, and
ADAIR, WILLIAM P., Cherokee
Reply of the Southern Cherokees to the Memorial of Certain Delegates from The Cherokee Nation. Washington: M'Gill and Witherow, 1866. pp. 1-12. Out of print.

The authors discuss the two antagonistic factions in the Cherokee Nation during the period 1830-1860 and describe each faction's position on the treaties of 1835, 1846, and 1865.

BOULANGER, TOM, Cree
An Indian Remembers: My Life as a Trapper in Northern Manitoba. Winnipeg, Manitoba: Peguis Publishers, 1971. 85 pp. Illus. $4.95.

Boulanger, born in 1901 in Manitoba, Canada, writes a story of his family and community life and of the hardships and pleasures of trapping, fishing, and trading.

BRONSON, RUTH MUSKRAT, Cherokee
Indians Are People Too. New York: Friendship Press, 1944. 184 pp. Out of print.

In a general discussion of twentieth-century Indians, reservation life, Indian values, family life, education, and leadership are covered.

BROOKS, BENJAMIN, *et al.*, Micmac
Legends of the Micmacs, ed. by Rev. Silas Tertius Rand. New York: Johnson Reprint Corp., 1971. 294 pp. $22.50.

This is a reprint of an 1894 book in which Rev. Rand presents his translation of a collection of 87 legends related to him in Micmac. Many of the Micmac narrators are cited. Rand's introduction discusses manners, customs, language, and literature of the Micmacs, a tribe living in New Brunswick.

BROWN, BETTY, Yana, see BAT'WĪ, SAM.

BROWN, CATHERINE, Cherokee
Memoirs of Catherine Brown, a Christian Indian of the Cherokee Nation, ed. by Rufus Anderson. Boston: Crocker and Brewster, 1825. 144 pp. Out of print.

Anderson's biography contains extracts from the diary and letters written by Catherine Brown, a Cherokee woman who was born about 1800 in Alabama. Her writings reflect her Christian education and training in mission schools.

BROWN, MARGARET WILEY, Cherokee, see OWL, MRS: SAMSON.

BUCHANAN, JIM, Coos
Coos Texts, ed. by Leo J. Frachtenberg. New York: AMS Press, Inc., 216 pp. $11.25.

Coos mythology narrated by Mr. Buchanan is presented in Coos and English texts (northwest United States). This is a reprint of Columbia Univ. Contributions to Anthropology, Vol. I, 1913.

BURNETTE, ROBERT, Sioux
The Tortured Americans, Englewood Cliffs, New Jersey: Prentice-Hall, Inc., 1971. 176 pp. Illus. $7.95.

A controversial version of contemporary Sioux politics in South Dakota and an attack on state and federal agencies concerned with Indian affairs, this book contains strongly biased statements and should be read in that light.

CALVIN, HEZEKIAH, Delaware, see ASHPO, SAMUEL.

CAMERON, DON; DEKINĀ´K!ᵘ; KATISHAN, *et al.,* Tlinget
Tlinget Myths and Texts, recorded by John Reed Swanton. New York: Johnson Reprint Corp. 451 pp. $18.00.

Eighty-eight myths recorded in English at Sitka and Wrangell, Alaska in 1904 and ten texts of speeches and songs given in both English and Tlinget are recorded in this book. It is a reprint of U. S. Bureau of American Ethnology, Bulletin 39, 1909.

CARDINAL, HAROLD, Cree
The Unjust Society: The Tragedy of Canada's Indians. Edmonton, Alberta: M. G. Hurtig, 1969. 171 pp. $2.75 paperbound.

The author discusses treaties, the Indian Act, Metis, whites who are legally Indians, full-bloods who are legally non-Indians, attitudes toward Indians, education, missionaries, bureaucracy, and denial of aboriginal rights to land ownership.

CASTRO, AMBROSIO A.; LOPEZ, RAFAEL; CHAVEZ, LUCAS, *et al.,* Yaqui
Yaqui Myths and Legends, collected by Ruth Warner Giddings. Tucson: Univ. of Arizona Press, 1959. 180 pp. Illus. $3.95.

This collection of Yaqui folktales from Sonora, Mexico and southern Arizona reflects beliefs and practices of the merged Yaqui-Catholic religion as well as a Yaqui conception of supernatural beings and animals with human feelings.

CHA-LA-PÍ, Navajo
Navajo Indian Poems: Translation from the Navajo, and Other Poems, as told to Hilda Faunce Wetherill. New York: Vantage Press, 1952. 53 pp. Out of print.

The poetry recorded here presents the activities of Navajo daily life.

CHAVEZ, LUCAS, Yaqui, see CASTRO, AMBROSIO.

CHIEF EAGLE, DALLAS, Sioux
Winter Count. Boulder, Colorado: Johnson Publishing Co., 1968. 230 pp. Illus. Out of print.

This historical novel about the Teton Sioux in the last quarter of the nineteenth century is primarily a military treatment based on Chief Eagle's interviews with tribal elders. It deals with the impact of non-Indian civilization upon American Indians.

CHIEF JOSEPH, Nez Perce
Chief Joseph's Own Story. Billings, Montana: Montana Indian Publications, 1972. 31 pp. Illus. $1.25 paperbound.

Chief Joseph recounts the events of the 1877 war between his tribe and the United States. He discusses the roles of the U. S. Indian agents and Army generals in the hostilities. This is a reprint of article in *North American Review,* Vol. CCLXIX, April, 1879. pp. 415-433.

CHIEF MEYERS, Cahuilla
"Chief Meyers" in *The Glory of Their Times: The Story of the Early Days of Baseball Told by the Men Who Played It,* as told to Lawrence S. Ritter. New York: The Macmillan Co., 1966. pp. 162-176. Illus. $7.95. Also paperbound: $2.50.

Chief Meyers, born in 1880, played baseball for the New York Giants from 1908 through 1915 and was traded to the Brooklyn Dodgers in 1916. In this narrative, Meyers recalls his experiences and acquaintances—Casey Stengel, Chief Bender, and Jim Thorpe among them—in the baseball world.

CHONA, MARIA, Papago
Autobiography of a Papago Woman, ed. by Ruth Underhill. Menasha, Wisconsin: The American Anthropological Association Memoirs, Vol. 46, 1936. 64 pp. Out of print.

Chona, 90 years of age, tells the story of her past and presents a picture of a Papago woman's role and status in the last quarter of the nineteenth and early twentieth centuries.

CLARENCE, Zuni, see ZUNI, FLORA.

CLARKE, PETER DOOYENTATE, Wyandott
Origin and Traditional History of the Wyandotts and Sketches of Other Indian Tribes of North America. Toronto: Hunter, Rose, and Co., 1870. 158 pp. Out of print.

This book is a history of the Wyandott Tribe, located in the Northeast since the early sixteenth century. It presents information on Tecumseh that had not been published before.

CLUTESI, GEORGE, Nootka
Son of Raven, Son of Deer. Sidney, British Columbia: Gray's Publishing, Ltd., 1967. 126 pp. Illus. by author. $5.95.

These twelve fables of the Tse-shaht people reveal various aspects of a rich culture. They are for teaching children the many wonders of nature, the importance of all living things, and the closeness of man to all animals, birds and sea creatures.

Potlatch. Sidney, British Columbia: Gray's Publishing, Ltd., 1969. 188 pp. Illus. by author. $5.95.

This is a day-by-day account of a British Columbian Indian winter festival. The ceremony, called a potlatch, is a feast accompanied by ritual gift-giving.

COHOE, WILLIAM, Cheyenne
A Cheyenne Sketchbook, with commentary by E. Adamson Hoebel and Karen Daniels Peterson. Norman: Univ. of Oklahoma Press, 1964. 96 pp. Illus. by author. Out of print.

Cohoe, one of 72 warriors from the Great Plains taken as prisoners to Fort Marion, Florida in 1875, has sketched scenes from his past life and his experiences as a prisoner. These drawings are in three groups: life on the plains, hunting; life on the plains, ceremonies; life at Fort Marion, prisoners of war.

COMOCK, Eskimo
The Story of Comock the Eskimo, as told to Robert Flaherty. New York: Simon and Schuster, Inc., 1968. 95 pp. Illus. $4.50. Also paperbound: Greenwich, Connecticut: Fawcett Publications, Inc., $.95.

Comock leads his starving family and two companions to a distant island rumored to be rich in game. Part of his family and one companion who survive the journey live a decade on the island and then eventually return to the mainland.

CONCHA, JOSEPH L., Taos Pueblo
Lonely Deer: Poems by a Pueblo Boy. Taos, New Mexico: Red Willow Society, 1969. 36 pp. Illus. by author. $1.50. Available from: Red Willow Society, Box 1184, Taos, N. M. 87571.

This booklet contains a collection of 34 poems by a Taos Pueblo boy, born in 1954 in New Mexico, with several color illustrations by the author.

CONFERENCE ON CALIFORNIA INDIAN EDUCATION, California tribes
Report of the First All-Indian Statewide Conference on California Indian Education: North Fork. Modesto: California Indian Education Association, Inc., 1967. 88 pp. Temporarily out of print.

This report by an all-Indian committee concerns itself primarily with ways in which the situation of the Indian children in the California school system can be improved. Other reports on CIEA conferences are also temporarily out of print. Query regarding new publication dates and prices from publisher: CIEA, Box 4095, Modesto, California 95352.

COON, BILL, Pomo, see POT, BOB.

COPWAY, GEORGE (KAH-GE-GA-GAH-BOWH),
Chippewa
Indian Life and Indian History: By an Indian Author.
Boston: Albert Colby and Co., Inc., 1860. 266 pp.
Out of print.

The author writes about Ojibway (Chippewa) history, culture, legends, language, and the impact of Christianity on Ojibway life. Included are several letters written to newspapers outlining the Indians' poor situation in America and plans for improving it. Also titled: *Traditional History and Characteristic Sketches of the Ojibway Nation.*

The Life, Letters, and Speeches of Kah-Ge-Ga-Gah-Bowh. New York: S. W. Benedict, 1850. 224 pp. Out of print.

This book contains a description of the culture of the Ojibway (Chippewa) as well as the author's own personal story. Included are two speeches on Indian affairs Copway delivered before two state legislatures. Also titled: *The Life, History, and Travels of Kah-Ge-Ga-Gah-Bowh* and *Recollections of a Forest Life.*

The Ojibway Conquest: A Tale of the Northwest.
New York: George P. Putnam, 1850. 91 pp. Out of print.

This poem, based on tradition, describes the constant warfare and last decisive battle between the Ojibway and Sioux in which the latter tribe was compelled to abandon its possessions east of the Mississippi River to the Ojibway.

Organization of a New Indian Territory, East of the Missouri River. New York: S. W. Benedict, 1850. 32 pp. Out of print.

Copway briefly reasons why Indians have not materially improved in America and then states a plan to save Indians from extinction. A sampling of letters commenting on the plan is included.

CORNPLANTER, JESSE J., Seneca
Legends of the Longhouse. Port Washington, New York: Ira J. Friedman, Inc., 1963. 218 pp. Illus. by author. $6.75.

This reprint of a 1938 edition contains a collection of the myths and legends of the Seneca Tribe which form the basis of the Longhouse religion and provide a guide to moral behavior.

COSTO, RUPERT, Cahuilla
Contributions and Achievements of the American Indian. San Francisco: The Indian Historian Press, 1973. Illus. $10.00. Also paperbound: $4.00.

The author brings together the evidence of the contributions and achievements of Indians in art and architecture, religion and philosophy, mathematics, medicine and health practice, plant use and agriculture, irrigation, literature and mythology.

CRASHING THUNDER, Winnebago
Crashing Thunder: The Autobiography of a Winnebago, ed. by Paul Radin. New York: Dover Publications, Inc., 1963. 91 pp. $1.25 paperbound.

A republication of a 1920 edition, this life story of a Winnebago man incorporates a great deal of information about the tribe's folklore and customs with a frank treatment of the author's life.

CROW-WING, Hopi
A Pueblo Indian Journal, 1920-21, ed. by Elsie Clews Parsons. New York: Kraus Reprint Co. 123 pp. Illus. Temporarily out of stock.

Crow-Wing's journal contains information on Hopi life (festivals, games, sports, marriages, weather and crop reports, details of appointments to public office, etc.) as well as details about contacts with Navajos and whites, the Hopi cultural setting, and other ethnological material. This is a reprint of Memoirs of the American Anthropological Association No. 32, 1925.

CUERO, DELPHINA, Southern Diegueño
The Autobiography of Delphia Cuero: A Diegueño Indian, as told to Florence C. Shipek. Banning, California: Malki Museum Press. 67 pp. $3.50 paperbound.

In the course of recording the struggle of a displaced Indian in modern society, Mrs. Cuero provides information about the traditional life of California Indians. Food gathering methods, hunting and fishing along the coastal regions, trade relations, leadership selection and role, ceremonial participation, and cultural change are discussed.

CULTEE, CHARLES, Chinook
Chinook Texts, translated and explained by Franz Boas. U. S. Bureau of American Ethnology, Bulletin 20. Washington: Government Printing Office, 1894. 278 pp. Out of print.

This is a collection of myths, tales, tribal beliefs and customs and two historical tales of this tribe located in Washington, narrated by Cultee. Chinook and English texts.

Kathlamet Texts, recorded and translated by Franz Boas. U. S. Bureau of American Ethnology, Bulletin 26. Washington: Government Printing Office, 1901. 261 pp. Out of print.

Myths and tales of the Kathlamet-speaking people located in Oregon are provided in text and translated forms.

CURLY, RIVER JUNCTION, Navajo, see CURLY, SLIM.

CURLY, SLIM; MITCHELL, FRANK; CURLY, RIVER JUNCTION, *et al.,* Navajo

Blessingway, ed. by Leland C. Wyman. Tucson: Univ. of Arizona Press, 1970. 660 pp. Illus. $19.50.

This book contains three versions of the Navajo Blessingway rite as told to Father Bernard Haile in 1931. It includes tables explaining major mythic motifs of the Blessingway, a rite concerned with peace and harmony. The illustrations include reproductions and symbols of Blessingway dry paintings.

CUSICK, DAVID, Tuscarora

Sketches of Ancient History of the Six Nations. Lewiston, New York: Printed for the author, 1827. 28 pp. Out of print.

The author recounts a native tale of the foundation of North America and the creation of the universe and gives an account of the Indian settlers of North America and the origin of the Five Nations, called the Longhouse, located in New York State.

DEKINĀ´K![u], Tlinget, see CAMERON, DON.

DELORIA, ELLA CARA, Sioux

Dakota Texts. American Ethnological Society Publications, Vol. XIV. New York: G. E. Stechert and Co., 1932. 279 pp. Out of print.

Teton Sioux tales from the Standing Rock (North and South Dakota), Pine Ridge (South Dakota), and Rosebud (South Dakota) reservations are transcribed in Sioux directly from storytellers who related them to the author. Each tale is accompanied by the author's translation, with notes on grammar and custom.

Speaking of Indians. New York: Friendship Press, 1944. 163 pp. Out of print.

This is an examination of the most significant elements in the life of a Sioux before white settlement. It discusses the social, religious, economic, and educational adjustments to a new way of life and the elements of the old way which persist in spite of the encroachments of another culture.

DELORIA, VINE, JR., Sioux

Custer Died for Your Sins: An Indian Manifesto. New York: The Macmillan Co. 1969. 279 pp. $3.95. Also paperbound: New York: Avon Books, $1.25.

Mr. Deloria writes of American Indians in today's world. He discusses the roles of treaties, government policies and agencies, the white man's law, missionaries, and anthropologists in contemporary Indian affairs.

God is Red. New York: Grosset and Dunlap, Inc., 1973. 376 pp. $7.95.

The author analyzes the religious crisis in contemporary American life and argues that Christianity has failed both in its theology and in its application to social issues. He calls for a complete change in our social and theological outlook and a return to the religious concepts of American Indians. In exploring events important to the Indian movement of the past decade, Mr. Deloria examines those concepts central to Indian religions.

We Talk, You Listen: New Tribes, New Turf. New York: The Macmillan Co., 1970. 227 pp. $5.95. Also paperbound: New York: Delta Books, $2.45.

The author discusses in a series of essays the meaning and consequences of the differences in world view between Indians (tribal) and whites (individualistic). He discusses his belief that white society must adopt a tribal-communal way of life if it is to survive in humanistic form.

DELORIA, VINE V., Sr., Sioux; **YOUNG BEAR, RAY**, Sauk and Fox; **JOHNSON, JAY RALPH**, Navajo, *et al.*
American Indian II, ed. by John Milton. Vermillion, South Dakota; Univ. of South Dakota Press, 1971. 199 pp. Illus. $3.50.

This collection of contemporary Indian writing and art includes a selection of poems by four poets, a section of a novel in progress, a legend, the works and comments of three Indian artists, and a personal reminiscence by Vine V. Deloria, Sr. An earlier volume edited by John Milton entitled *The American Indian Speaks* (Univ. of South Dakota Press, 1969) which is now out of print presents a collection of contemporary writing and painting by Indians primarily from the western half of the country.

DESERONTYOU, JOHN, Mohawk

A Mohawk Form of Ritual Condolence: 1782, translated by John Napoleon Brinton Hewitt. New York: Museum of the American Indian, Heye Foundation, 1928. 23 pp. $.75 paperbound.

Customary forms of Mohawk sacred rituals and chants are presented as they were used in the late eighteenth century.

DOCKSTADER, FREDERICK J., Oneida

The American Indian in Graduate Studies. New York: Museum of the American Indian, Heye Foundation, 1956. 399 pp. $5.00 paperbound.

Listed here are over 3,500 theses and dissertations from colleges throughout North America. A supplementary volume is now in progress. The theses deal with the Indian tribes of North, Central, and South America, and the Eskimos of the Arctic.

Indian Art in America: The Arts and Crafts of the North American Indian. Greenwich, Connecticut: New York Graphic Society, 1966. 224 pp. Illus. $27.50. Also: $14.95 hardbound.

North American Indian art is surveyed from its earliest known examples to the present day.

Indian Art in Middle America. Greenwich, Connecticut: New York Graphic Society, 1964. 224 pp. Illus. $27.50.

This survey of ancient and historic aboriginal art includes objects from northern Mexico to southern Panama, including the West Indies.

Indian Art in South America: Pre-Columbian and Contemporary Arts and Crafts. Greenwich, Connecticut: New York Graphic Society, 1967. 225 pp. Illus. $27.50.

Here Mr. Dockstader surveys the aboriginal art of South America from Colombia to Argentina, including contemporary cultures as well as ancient ones.

The Kachina and the White Man: The Influences of the White Culture on the Hopi Kachina Cult. Bloomfield Hills, Michigan: Cranbrook Institute of Science, Bulletin No. 35, 1954. 204 pp. Illus. by author. $6.00. Available from: Museum of the American Indian, Broadway at 155th Street, New York, New York 10032.

This work studies the origins and development of Hopi (and Zuni) ceremonials and the degree to which they have been changed because of outside cultural influences.

Pre-Columbian Art and Later Indian Tribal Arts, with Ferdinand Anton. New York: Harry N. Abrams, Inc., 1968. 264 pp. Illus. $8.95.

In this work, the authors examine pre-Columbian art and later Indian tribal arts in the Western Hemisphere, from the Arctic to the Antarctic.

DOZIER, EDWARD P., Santa Clara Pueblo

Hano, A Tewa Community in Arizona. New York: Holt, Rinehart and Winston, 1966. 104 pp. $2.50 paperbound.

Dr. Dozier details the history, development, and present situation of one Indian community in Arizona.

Pueblo Indians of North America. New York: Holt, Rinehart and Winston, 1970. 192 pp. $4.50 paperbound.

This is an historical and cultural account of approximately twenty Pueblo Indian villages in the Southwest, from their origins to the present, told from the Indian point of view.

"Two Examples of Linguistic Acculturation: The Yaqui of Sonora and Arizona and the Tewa of New Mexico," in *Language in Culture and Society,* ed. by Dell Hymes. New York: Harper and Row, 1964. pp. 509-520. $14.95.

The adjustments of two Indian languages due to their contacts with other cultures are treated here.

DUCHENEAUX, KAREN, Sioux, see KICKINGBIRD, KIRKE.

DUMONT, ROBERT V., JR., Assiniboine

Formal Education in an American Indian Community. Co-authored by Murray L. and Rosalie H. Wax. Social Problems Monograph No. 1. Kalamazoo, Michigan: The Society for the Study of Social Problems, 1964. 126 pp. Out of print.

The relationship between a Sioux community in South Dakota and its school is traced and documented through contemporary observations made during visits to federal schools. The author argues that schools serving Indian communities should be controlled by Indians.

"Learning English and How to Be Silent: Studies in Sioux and Cherokee Classrooms," in *Functions of Language,* ed. by Courtney B. Cazden, Vera P. Johns, and Dell Hymes. New York: Teachers College Press, 1972. pp. 344-369. $9.50. Also paperbound: $5.95.

This report of field work done in 1967 in Oklahoma and North Dakota discusses the phenomenon of student silence in Cherokee and Sioux classrooms.

EASTMAN, CHARLES ALEXANDER (OHIYESA), Sioux

From the Deep Woods to Civilization: Chapters in the Autobiography of an Indian. Boston: Little, Brown and Co., 1916. 206 pp. Illus. Out of print.

Dr. Eastman tells of his life from his fifteenth year to the second decade of the twentieth century. His story includes discussion of his college life, medical training, practice of medicine, and work among Indians.

Indian Boyhood. New York: Dover Publications, Inc., 1971. 247 pp. Illus. $2.00 paperbound.

Eastman's first book, published in 1902, contains reminiscences of the author's first 15 years and includes the customs, traditions, religion, legends, and history of the Santee Sioux prior to the reservation period. Sentiments expressed in the first paragraph of the dedication are unworthy of the rest of the book.

Indian Scout Talks: A Guide for Boy Scouts and Camp Fire Girls. Boston: Little, Brown and Co., 1914. 190 pp. Out of print.

Chapters by Eastman include information about the ways Indians trained for life close to nature, befriended animals, "read" footprints, trapped, fished, made and handled canoes. General information about Indian symbols, sign language, pictography and ceremonies is also included.

The Indian Today: the Past and Future of the First American. Garden City, New York: Doubleday, 1915. 185 pp. Out of print.

The author discusses the past up to the early twentieth century and makes some predictions for the future.

Old Indian Days. Rapid City, South Dakota: Fenwyn Press, 1970. 279 pp. Illus. $2.95. Available from: Black Hill Books, 511 St. Joe Street, Rapid City, South Dakota 57701.

This reprint of a 1907 book discusses the daily life of Antelope, a young Sioux who wishes to be a noted warrior among his people, and the life of Winoma and other women who demonstrate Sioux virtues and ideals.

Red Hunters and the Animal People. New York: Harper and Brothers, 1904. 248 pp. Out of print.

Stories based on the experiences and observations of Sioux hunters in the Northwest before 1870 are presented along with fables, songs, and the life-stories of animals according to Sioux legend.

Soul of an Indian: An Interpretation. Rapid City, South Dakota: Fenwyn Press, 1970. 170 pp. $2.95 paperbound. Available from: Black Hill Books, 511 St. Joe Street, Rapid City, South Dakota 57701.

This is a reprint of 1911 book in which Eastman presents the religious life of Indians as it was before the advent of white men. He discusses the place of the family, ceremonial and symbolic worship, moral code, and unwritten scriptures in Indian religions. Also available: Johnson Reprint Corp., $7.50.

EN-ME-GAH-BOWH, Chippewa

En-me-Gah-bowh's Story: An Account of Disturbances of Chippewa Indians at Gull Lake in 1857 and 1862 and Their Removal in 1868. Minneapolis, Minnesota: Woman's Auxiliary, St. Barnabas Hospital, 1904. 56 pp. Out of print.

In this booklet, written when he was 86, the author gives an account of an Indian disturbance with whites in 1857 given him by an Indian eyewitness. A personal account of events in 1862 and 1868 when the Chippewa were removed to White Earth, Minnesota is included, along with a chapter on the Sioux-Chippewa peace treaty.

ERICKSON, SHEILA, Carrier

NOTICE: This Is an Indian Reserve, ed. by Kent Gooderham. Toronto: Griffin House Publishers, 1972. 83 pp. Illus. $4.50 paperbound.

This is a collection of photographs of contemporary Canadian Indian reservation life with poetry by Sheila Erickson, who belongs to the Carrier Tribe located in northeastern British Columbia.

FADDEN, RAY (AREN AKWEKS), Mohawk

History of the Oneida Nation. Hogansburg, New York: Akwesasne Mohawk Counselor Organization. Unpaged. Illus. $1.25 paperbound. Available from: Ray Fadden, Six Nations Indian Museum, Onchiota, New York 12968.

This history of the Oneidas, beginning with the first contacts with white men in 1535, generally discusses Iroquois history during the colonial period and American Revolution. The author discusses the removal of the tribe to Wisconsin in 1823 and gives a brief history of them since their removal there. Also included are biographies of past and present-day Oneida leaders. Write the Six Nations Museum for further publications by Ray Fadden.

Migration of the Iroquois. Rooseveltown, New York: White Roots of Peace, 1972. 32 pp. $.50 paperbound. Order from: White Roots of Peace, Mohawk Nation at Akwesasne, via Rooseveltown, N. Y. 13683.

This story is about the Hotinonsonni, or the People of the Longhouse, as recorded on a beaded belt which can be seen at the Six Nations Museum in Onchiota, New York.

FARMER'S BROTHER, Seneca, see RED JACKET.

FIELDING, FIDELIA A. H., Mohegan-Pequot
Native Tribes and Dialects of Connecticut: A Mohegan-Pequot Diary, ed. by Frank G. Speck, U. S. Bureau of American Ethnology, Forty-third Annual Report. Washington: Government Printing Office 1928. pp. 199-287. Illus. Out of print.

The diary of Mrs. Fielding, born in 1827 in Connecticut, written in Mohegan-Pequot (with an English translation included) covers December 20, 1902 to January 7, 1905. The diary is accompanied by a history of the Mohegan-Pequot Tribe and information about Mrs. Fielding. The appendix includes Mohegan folk tales and ethnological material.

FLYING CLOUD, CHIEF
(FRANCIS BENJAMIN ZAHN), Sioux
The Crimson Carnage of Wounded Knee. Bottineau, North Dakota: Edward A. Milligan, 1967. 12 pp. $1.00 paperbound.

This is the story of the 1890 massacre at Wounded Knee, South Dakota, as told to the author by White Lance and Dewey Beard, two of the survivors.

FLYING HAWK, Sioux
Firewater and Forked Tongues: A Sioux Chief Interprets U. S. History, as told to M. I. McCreight. Pasadena, California: Trail's End Publishing Co., Inc., 1947. Out of print.

Flying Hawk, born about 1852, discusses the history of the United States from the arrival of the first white man. Included are short narratives about Flying Hawk himself, Indian philosophy, well-known Indians, and battles between Indians and non-Indians.

FOLSOM, ISRAEL, Choctaw, see
PITCHLYNN, PETER PERKINS.

FOLSOM-DICKERSON, W. E. S., Choctaw
Cliff Dwellers. San Antonio, Texas: The Naylor Co., 1968. 164 pp. Illus. $4.95.

The author narrates a contemporary exploration of the Southwest and Indian architectural ruins. Some reasons for the cliff dwellers' disappearance are given.

The White Path. San Antonio, Texas: The Naylor Co., 1965. 148 pp. Illus. $4.95.

A study of the Alabama Tribe of eastern Texas, this book discusses the religion, concepts of nature, material traits, industries, language, social organization, government, and other concepts of the tribe.

FORBES, JACK D., Powhatan
Apache, Navaho, and Spaniard. Norman: Univ. of Oklahoma Press, 1960. 340 pp. Illus. $7.95. Also paperbound: $2.95.

The author traces the history of the Southern Athapascans and their relations with other Indians and with the Spanish Empire from the first written records (about 1540) until 1698.

Warriors of the Colorado: The Yumas of the Quechan Nation and Their Neighbors. Norman: Univ. of Oklahoma Press, 1965. 378 pp. Illus. $8.95.

The author attempts to gather together all of the material relating to the past of a Colorado River society (Quechan [Yuma] Nation) in order to illustrate the history of an important tribal group. The reconstruction sheds light on the development of many groups bordering the Quechans, including the Kamias, Cocopas, Halchidhomas, Mohaves, Maricopas, Pimas and Papagos.

Native Americans of California and Nevada: A Handbook. Healdsburg, California: Naturegraph Publishers, 1969. 202 pp. Illus. $3.95 paperbound.

This handbook is designed to provide an introduction to the evolution of Indian peoples in California and Nevada in light of historical-cultural experiences that have shaped present-day conditions of Indian communities and individuals. The book also is designed to provide an introduction to basic concepts relating to Indian studies and to the multi-cultural, community-relevant approach to Indian education.

FORBES, JACK D., Powhatan, see ANONYMOUS, NEVADA INDIANS.

FREDERICKS, OSWALD WHITE BEAR, Hopi

Book of the Hopi, text by Frank Waters. New York: The Viking Press, Inc., 1963. 448 pp. Illus. by author. $12.50. Also paperbound: New York: Ballantine Books. $1.25.

These drawings and source materials provide an account of Hopi historical and religious world views as interpreted by a Hopi artist in collaboration with a non-Indian novelist.

FRY, MAGGIE CULVER, Cherokee

The Umbilical Cord. Chicago: Windfall Press, 1971. 48 pp.

The subject matter of these 47 poems by Mrs. Fry, born in 1900 in Oklahoma, are drawn from everyday events, memories, and her Indian heritage.

The Witch Deer: Poems of the Oklahoma Indians. Claremont, Oklahoma: By the Author, 1954. 40 pp. Illus. Temporarily out of print. Contact Mrs. Fry: Rt. 7, Box 165, Claremont, Okla. 74017.

The 31 poems in this collection are based on authentic legends, customs, and history of Oklahoma Indians.

GABOURIE, FRED WHITEDEER, Seneca

Justice and the Urban American Indian. Sherman Oaks, California: Merdler and Gabourie Law Firm, 1971. 17 pp. $2.50. Available from: Mr. Fred W. Gabourie, 9601 Wilshire Blvd., Suite 340, Beverly Hills, California 90212.

The author discusses problems peculiar to Indians who move from rural Indian areas, reservations, and communities to live in urban areas.

GAHUNI, Cherokee, see SWIMMER, GAHUNI, INÂ´LĬ, *et al.*, Cherokee.

GARLAND, SAMUEL, Choctaw, see PITCHLYNN, PETER PERKINS.

GEORGE, HAMILTON, Nootka, see TOM.

GERONIMO, Apache
Geronimo's Story of His Life, as told to and edited by Steven Melvil Barrett. Newly edited by Frederick W. Turner III. New York. E. P. Dutton & Co., Inc., 1970. 190 pp. Illus. $7.95. Also paperbound: New York: Ballantine Books. $1.25.

While Geronimo was imprisoned at Fort Sill, Oklahoma Territory, he dictated the story of his life, giving both a cultural and an historical account of the Apaches to Mr. Barrett.

GLADSTONE, WILLY, Bella Bella
Bella Bella Texts, ed. by Franz Boas. New York: AMS Press, Inc. $15.00.

Bella Bella tales as narrated by Mr. Gladstone are presented in Bella Bella and English texts (British Columbia). This is a reprint of Columbia Univ. Contributions to Anthropology, Vol. V, 1928.

GOODBIRD, EDWARD, Hidatsa
Goodbird, The Indian: His Story, ed. by Gilbert L. Wilson. New York: Fleming H. Revell Co., 1914. 80 pp. Illus. Out of print.

Born about 1869, Goodbird relates information about his birth, childhood, schooling in a mission, and religious beliefs to Mr. Wilson in 1913. Raised as a Christian, Goodbird extolls the role of Christianity in Indian life.

GORDON, SALLY, Cherokee, see OWL, MRS. SAMSON.

GRIFFIS, JOSEPH K. (CHIEF TAHAN), Osage
Indian Circle Stories. Burlington, Vermont: Free Press Printing Co., 1928. 138 pp. Out of print.

These stories, heard by the author as he grew to manhood, were told by the storytellers of the Kiowa, Cherokee, Choctaw, and Malecite tribes.

Tahan: Out of Savagery into Civilization. New York: George B. Doran Co., 1915. 263 pp. Out of print.

This autobiography of an Osage, who was born in the middle of the nineteenth century, covers his varied background as warrior, medicine man, outlaw, scout, Salvation Army captain, clergyman, and scholar.

GRISDALE, ALEX, Chippewa

Wild Drums: Tales and Legends of the Plains Indians, as told to Nan Shipley. Winnipeg, Manitoba: Peguis Publishers, 1972. 78 pp. Illus. $4.95.

Seventy-seven-year-old Grisdale presents a collection of stories he has been told by elderly native people of the Plains. The stories of individual and tribal courage depict life among the Assiniboines, Cree, Sioux, Saulteaux and Blackfeet as it was before the arrival of Europeans. A short autobiography is included.

HENSON, LANCE, Cheyenne

Keeper of Arrows: Poems for the Cheyenne. Chickasha, Oklahoma: Renaissance Press, 1971. Unpaged. $2.00 paperbound. Available from Renaissance Press, 1112 Kansas, Chickasha, Okla. 73018.

Lance Henson, born in Washington, D.C. in 1944 and raised by grandparents in Texas and Oklahoma, has created over 50 poems reflecting "the aesthetics of his own Cheyenne culture."

HEWITT, JOHN NAPOLEON BRINTON, Tuscarora

Articles in the *Handbook of the American Indians North of Mexico,* ed. by Frederick Webb Hodge. St. Clair Shores, Michigan: Scholarly Press, 1968. 2 vols. $82.50.

Hewitt contributed articles to this handbook, originally published in 1912, which gives brief descriptions of linguistic stocks, confederacies, tribes, tribal divisions, settlements known to history or tradition, and discusses the origins or derivations of names where they are known.

Iroquois Cosmology, in U. S. Bureau of American Ethnology, Twenty-first Annual Report. Washington: Government Printing Office, 1904. pp. 127-339. Illus. Out of print.

Onondaga, Seneca, and Mohawk versions of Iroquois cosmology are given here with original texts and English translations.

Journal of Rudolph Friedrich Kurz, ed. by Hewitt, U. S. Bureau of American Ethnology, Bulletin 115. Washington: Government Printing Office, 1937 382 pp. Out of print.

This account of Kurz' experiences among fur traders and American Indians on the Mississippi and the upper Missouri Rivers covers the years from 1846 to 1852.

HOFFMAN, JOSEPH, Apache, see **PRINCE, ANNA.**

HOPKINS, SARAH WINNEMUCCA, Paiute
Life Among the Paiutes: Their Wrongs and Claims, ed. by Mrs. Horace Mann. Bishop, California: Chalfant Press, Inc., 1969. $5.95 paperbound.

Mrs. Hopkins, born about 1844 in Nevada, describes her life as well as her tribe's culture and history before and after contact with whites. Her purpose in writing the book was to acquaint the public with the injustices the Paiute bands of Nevada had suffered. This is a photographic reproduction of an 1883 original.

HOWARD, VICTORIA, Clackamas Chinook
Clackamas Chinook Texts, ed. by Melville Jacobs. Bloomington, Indiana: Indiana Univ. Research Center in Anthropology, Folklore, and Linguistics, 1958. 2 vols. 292 pp. Out of print.

Songs and oral literature narrated and translated by Mrs. Howard are presented in Clackamas Chinook and English texts (northwest United States).

HOWLING WOLF, Cheyenne
Howling Wolf: A Cheyenne Warrior's Graphic Interpretation of His People, text by Karen Daniels Petersen. Palo Alto: American West Publishing Co., 1968. 64 pp. Illus. by author. Out of print.

Sketches done by Howling Wolf while being held prisoner at Fort Marion in Florida from 1875 to 1878 tell the story of his people.

HOWLING WOLF, Cheyenne, and **ZO-TOM,** Kiowa
1877: Plains Indian Sketch Books of Zo-Tom and Howling Wolf, ed. by Dorothy Dunn. Flagstaff, Arizona: Northland Press, 1969. Unpaged. Illus. by authors. $35.00.

The sketch books of Howling Wolf and Zo-Tom, two Plains Indians who were prisoners in Fort Marion, Florida, are reproduced in this one volume. The drawings, made around 1877, contain scenes of Indian life on the Plains. The story of the sketch books and how they became public is told in the Introduction.

HUDSON, JOHN B., Kalapuya
Kalapuya Texts: Part I, Santiam Kalapuya Ethnologic Texts and *Part II, Santiam Kalapuya Myth Texts*, ed. by Melville Jacobs. Univ. of Washington Publications in Anthropology, Vol. XI. Seattle: Univ. of Washington, 1945. pp. 3-142. Out of print.

Ninety-two short descriptions of various facets of Kalapuya culture are narrated and translated by Mr. Hudson. Both Kalapuya and English texts are provided. Kalapuya myths, narrated and translated by Mr. Hudson, are presented in Kalapuya and English texts (northwest United States).

HUM-ISHU-MA (MOURNING DOVE), Okanogan
Co-ge-we-a, The Half-Blood: A Depiction of the Great Montana Cattle Range, as told to Sho-pow-tan. Boston: The Four Seas Co., 1927. 302 pp. Out of print.

This fictional narrative, based on Indian characters from real life, pictures the closing days of the great cattle range, and the decadence of its reigning head, the cowboy.

Coyote Stories, ed. by Heister Dean Guie Caldwell. Caldwell, Idaho: Caxton Printers Ltd., 1933. 228 pp. Illus. Out of print.

Hum-ishu-ma relates stories and legends of the Okanogan Indians, a Pacific Northwest tribe.

HUNT, JOE, Klikitat
Northwest Sahaptin Texts, ed. by Melville Jacobs. Univ. of Washington Publications in Anthropology, Vol. II, No. 6. Seattle: Univ. of Washington, 1929. Illus. 77 pp. $2.50 paperbound.

Thirteen traditional folk tales narrated by Mr. Hunt recall the customs and mythology of Klikitat culture. Klikitat and English texts are provided.

HUNTER, LOIS MARIE, Shinnecock
The Shinnecock Indians. Islip, New York: Buys Brothers, 1952. 90 pp. Out of print.

A descendant of Sachem Nowedonah tells the story of the Shinnecocks before and after contact with the white man.

HUNTINGTON, JAMES, Athabascan
On the Edge of Nowhere, as told to Lawrence Elliott.
New York: Crown Publishers, Inc., 1966. 183 pp. $4.50.

The author, born in Hughes, Alaska, in 1916, describes his parents, raising his sisters and brothers, daily life on the tundra, dogsled races, and his adulthood.

HYDE, VILLIANA, Luiseño
An Introduction to the Luiseño Language, ed. by Ronald W. Langacker. Banning, California: Malki Museum Press, 1971. 236 pp. $4.50 paperbound.

This book contains a grammar of a southern California Indian language. It offers the general public the opportunity to study an American Indian language, acquaints linguists and anthropologists with a non-Indo-European language, and serves as a teaching aid for the Indian community.

INÂ′LĬ, Cherokee, see SWIMMER; GAHUNI;
INÂ′LĬ, *et al.,* Cherokee.

INDIAN CHILDREN OF BRITISH COLUMBIA
Tales from the Longhouse. Sidney, British Columbia: Gray's Publishing, Ltd., 1973. 112 pp. $4.95.

Indian students living on Vancouver Island and in the village of Kingcome Inlet on the British Columbia coast gathered these stories and legends from older relatives over a six-year period. The stories are from the various Indian bands in British Columbia and are arranged under such headings as origins, power, nature, crafts, customs, animals, birds and legends.

INDIANS OF ALL TRIBES
Alcatraz Is Not an Island, ed. by Peter Blue Cloud.
Berkeley, California: Wingbow Press, 1972. 107 pp. Illus. $3.95 paperbound. Available from Book People, 2940 Seventh Street, Berkeley, California 94710.

This collection of documents (letters, press conferences, Alcatraz newsletters, government papers), thoughts, photographs, art, and poetry gives a history of the time when representatives of many Indian tribes occupied Alcatraz Island, near San Francisco, California from November 20, 1969 to June 11, 1971.

INO:LI (BLACK FOX), Cherokee

Chronicles of Wolftown: Social Documents of the North Carolina Cherokees, 1850-1862, ed. by Anna Gritts Kilpatrick and Jack Frederick Kilpatrick. U. S. Bureau of American Ethnology, Bulletin 196, Anthropological Papers, No. 75. Washington: Government Printing Office, 1966. pp. 5-111. Out of print.

The Ino:li papers contain documents pertaining to the civic affairs and cultural climate of Wolftown, the easternmost of the communities of the North Carolina Cherokees. Cherokee and English texts.

INSTITUTE OF AMERICAN INDIAN ARTS STUDENTS

Anthology of Poetry and Verse. Washington: U. S. Department of the Interior, Bureau of Indian Affairs, 1965. 27 pp. $.25 paperbound. Available from: Institute of American Indian Arts, Cerrillos Road, Santa Fe, New Mexico 87501.

Twenty-four selections by students in creative writing classes and clubs during the first three years of operation (1962-1965) of the Institute are included in this pamphlet.

The Whispering Winds: Poetry by Young American Indians, ed. by Terry Allen. Garden City, New York: Doubleday and Co., Inc., 1972. 128 pp. $1.95 paperbound.

Written by students at the Institute of American Indian Arts in Santa Fe, New Mexico, these poems cover such varied themes as Indian lore, the Vietnam War, childhood memories, thirst and loneliness. A brief biography of each poet precedes his or her poems.

IROQUOIS LEAGUE OF NATIONS

The Great Law of Peace of the Longhouse People. Rooseveltown, New York: White Roots of Peace, 1971. Unpaged. Illus. $1.00 paperbound. Order from: White Roots of Peace, Mohawk Nation at Akwesasne, via Rooseveltown, New York 13683.

This is a translation of the Great Law, given to the Iroquois Indians centuries ago and still operative today, which unified and governed six nations of Indians who did not speak the same language. Illustrations are by John Fadden, Mohawk.

ISAAC, Haida, see STEVENS, TOM.

JACOBS, PETER (PAH-TAH-SE-GA), Chippewa
Journal of the Reverend Peter Jacobs from Rice Lake to the Hudson's Bay Territory and Returning, Commencing May, 1852: With a Brief Account of His Life. Toronto: Anson Green, 1853. 32 pp. Out of print.

This journal, which covers several months of Jacobs' missionary activities, contains a biting attack on Indian religion and values. A short history of Wesleyan Mission in the Hudson Bay Territories is also included.

JAMES, BILL, Pomo, see POT, BOB.

JAMES, HERMAN, PARRISH, ESSIE; ANTONE, DAVID, *et al.,* Kashaya
Kashaya Texts, ed. by Robert L. Oswalt, Univ. of California Publications in Linguistics, Vol. 36. Berkeley: Univ. of California Press, 1964. 340 pp. Illus. Out of print.

Traditional stories, myths, tales of the supernatural, and folk history narrated by the main informants, Parrish and James, are recorded and translated in this collection. Both Kashaya and English texts are given.

JOHNSON, CHIEF ELIAS, Tuscarora
Legends, Traditions, and Laws of the Iroquois, or Six Nations, and History of the Tuscarora Indians. Lockport, New York: Union Publishing Co., 1881. 234 pp. Out of print.

The author provides a history of the Tuscarora Indians in North Carolina and New York. He discusses the tribe's relationships with the United States and includes some general information about Iroquois culture, history and legends. The first few chapters contain an attack on bigotry, intolerance, and racial prejudice.

JOHNSON, E. PAULINE (TEKAHIONWAKE), Mohawk
Flint and Feather: The Complete Poems of E. Pauline Johnson. Don Mills, Ontario: Paperjacks, 1972. 164 pp. $1.25 paperbound.

An introduction and biographical sketch accompany the poems, which are divided into three parts: "The White Wampum," "Canadian Born," (both formerly published as separate books), and a miscellaneous collection.

Legends of Vancouver. Toronto: McClelland and Stewart, 1920. Illus. Out of print.

Most of the legends in this book were told to Pauline Johnson by Chief Joe Capilano of Vancouver. A biographical note accompanies the legends.

JOHNSON, FRANCES, Takelma

Takelma Texts, ed. by Edward Sapir. Univ. of Pennsylvania Anthropological Publications of the University Museum, Vol. 11, No. 1. Philadelphia: University Museum, 1909. pp. 1-267. Out of print.

These texts contain the myths, customs, personal narratives and medical formulas collected from Frances Johnson during 1906 in western Oregon. Takelma and English texts and Takelma-English vocabularies are included.

JOHNSON, JAY RALPH, Navajo, see DELORIA, VINE V., Sr.

JOHNSTON, PATRONELLA, Chippewa

Tales of Nokomis, Toronto: Charles J. Musson, Ltd., 1970. 65 pp. Illus. $4.95.

The author, who runs a boarding house for young Indians in Toronto, recounts 17 legends to teach them the culture of her tribe. Color illustrations by Francis Kagige, a Chippewa, are included.

JONES, BILL; BLACKBIRD; WATCHES ALL, *et al.,* Gros Ventre

Gros Ventre Myths and Tales, ed. by A. L. Kroeber. Anthropological Papers, American Museum of Natural History Vol. 1, Part 3. New York: American Museum of Natural History, 1907. pp. 55-139. Out of print.

Bill Jones and six other informants from the Fort Belknap Reservation in Montana narrate 30 myths and 20 tales representing important stories of the tribe.

JONES, The Rev. PETER (KAH-KE-WA-QUO-NA-BY), Chippewa

Life and Journals of Kah-Ke-Wa-Quo-Na-By. Toronto: Anson Green, 1860. 424 pp. Out of print.

Accompanied by a brief autobiography, Rev. Jones' journals cover his travels and missionary activities among Canadian Ojibways (Chippewas) and other tribes from 1825-1855.

History of the Ojebway Indians: with Especial Reference to Their Conversion to Christianity. London: A. W. Bennett, 1861. 278 pp. Illus. Out of print.

This history of the Ojibway (Chippewa) Tribe in Canada includes commentary on the impact of white culture on Indians. The role of Christianity in Chippewa life is extolled by the author.

JOSEPHS, NOEL, Passamaquoddy, see
JOSEPHS, TOMAH.

JOSEPHS, TOMAH and **JOSEPHS, NOEL**, Passamaquoddy, **NEPTUNE, NOEL**, Penobscot, *et al.*
The Algonquin Legends of New England; or Myths and Folk Lore of the Micmac, Passamaquoddy, and Penobscot Tribes. Boston: Houghton Mifflin and Co., 1884. 379 pp. Illus. Out of print.

Myths, legends and folklore of the Algonquian Indians of New England, the Passamaquoddys and Penobscots of Maine and the Micmacs of New Brunswick, are included in this collection. Many of the tales specify the name of the narrator. An introductory essay points up the curious coincidences between the myths and tales of the northeastern Algonquians and those of the Norsemen.

JOSIE, EDITH, Loucheaux
Here Are the News. Toronto: Clarke, Irwin and Co., Ltd., 1966. 135 pp. Illus. $3.95.

This book contains the newspaper columns of Edith Josie which have appeared in the *Whitehorse Star* since the fall of 1962. She writes of the Indian village of Old Crow located on the banks of the Porcupine River inside the Arctic Circle. Her accounts of trapping, fishing, incoming planes, and dogsled races reflect what is considered newsworthy in Old Crow. The articles also record a way of life that is gradually being changed by contact with the outside world.

KABOTIE, FRED, Hopi
Design from the Ancient Mimbreños: With a Hopi Interpretation. San Francisco: Grabhorn Press, 1949. 83 pp. Illus. Out of print.

Thirty-eight illustrations from the pottery of the Mimbres (an ancient people of southwest New Mexico) accompany the author's interpretation of the life forms and geometric designs based on his knowledge of Hopi life and culture. A short history about the Mimbres introduces the illustrations.

KATCHONGVA, DAN, Hopi
Hopi: A Message for All People. Rooseveltown, New York: White Roots of Peace, 1973. 24 pp. Illus. $1.00 paperbound. Available from: *Akwesasne Notes,* Mohawk Nation, via Rooseveltown, New York 13683.

The author's message is that if Hopi teachings, prophecies, and ceremonial duties are doomed, the whole world will be destroyed. He describes the attempts of Hopi traditionalists to preserve Hopi land and a way of life while under constant attack from white men and tribal officials.

KATISHAN, Tlinget, see CAMERON, DON.

KAYWAYKLA, JAMES, Apache
In the Days of Victorio: Recollections of a Warm Springs Apache, told to Eve Ball. Tucson: Univ. of Arizona Press, 1970. 222 pp. Illus. $6.50. Also paperbound: $4.95.

The author, born about 1873, tells of his youth in the Southwest during a time in which Apache families are driven from their reservations, hunted like animals, and eventually herded aboard a train and shipped to Florida prisons in 1886. Kaywaykla also includes information on Apache daily life.

KENNEDY, DAN (OCHANKUGAHE), Assiniboine
Recollections of an Assiniboine Chief, ed. by James R. Stevens. Toronto: McClelland and Stewart, Ltd., 1972. 160 pp. Illus. $7.95.

In a series of stories, 100-year-old Kennedy reminisces about the history of his tribe in Saskatchewan (Canada). He discusses the effects on his tribe of the disappearance of buffalo and the appearance of railroads. He remembers Assiniboine leaders, encounters with white settlers, the Ghost Dance religion, the U. S. military massacre at Wounded Knee, and the Sundance. He also includes information on the struggle of the Assiniboines to adjust to an alien culture and life on reservations.

KENOI, SAMUEL E., Apache
"A Chiricahua Apache's Account of the Geronimo Campaign of 1886," ed. by M. E. Opler. *New Mexico Historical Review* Vol. 13, No. 4. October, 1938. pp. 360-386. Out of print.

Kenoi's narrative dealing with the 1885-1886 campaign to capture the Chiricahua leader, Geronimo, credits Charles Martine and Kaitah for locating Geronimo and inducing him to surrender. The narrative presents Geronimo as an "old trouble maker."

KICKINGBIRD, KIRKE, Kiowa and
DUCHENEAUX, KAREN, Sioux
One Hundred Million Acres. New York: The Macmillan Co., 1973. 240 pp. $6.95.

The authors review disputes over Indian ownership of approximately 100 million acres of land (including tribal and individually-owned lands, the Alaska land settlement, submarginal and surplus federal lands, and terminated and non-federal lands). A number of Indian land-claim cases are discussed against the background of the social, historical, and legal significance of the cases. The last chapter presents proposals for restoring land to Indian ownership.

KILPATRICK, JACK FREDERICK, Cherokee
Sequoyah of Earth and Intellect. Austin, Texas: The Encino Press, 1965. 25 pp. Out of print.

This biographical essay about Sequoyah, a Cherokee, includes information from *The Wahnenauhi Manuscript* written by a granddaughter of Major Lowrey, cousin of Sequoyah. It gives one version of how Sequoyah obtained the concept of his syllabary.

KILPATRICK, JACK FREDERICK and
KILPATRICK, ANNA GRITTS, Cherokee
Friends of Thunder: Folktales of the Oklahoma Cherokees, translated and edited by the Kilpatricks. Dallas: Southern Methodist Univ. Press, 1964. 197 pp. Out of print.

These myths and tales reflect the life and thought of the Cherokee people of Oklahoma. A chapter of transcribed tapes contains information on the religion, social structure, amusements and patterns of thought of the Cherokees, past and present. A list of the narrators is provided.

Run Toward the Nightland: Magic of the Oklahoma Cherokees, ed. by the Kilpatricks. Dallas: Southern Methodist Univ. Press, 1967. 212 pp. $5.00.

Medicine and magic rituals, with melodies and words, of the Oklahoma Cherokees are translated in this volume.

The Shadow of Sequoyah: Social Documents of the Cherokees, 1862-1964, trans. and ed. by the Kilpatricks. Norman: Univ. of Oklahoma Press, 1965. 129 pp. Illus. $5.95.

These Cherokee documents (letters, minutes of meetings, committee reports, and private memoranda) cover diverse subjects over a 100-year period.

Walk in Your Soul: Love Incantations of the Oklahoma Cherokees, ed. by the Kilpatricks. Dallas: Southern Methodist Univ. Press, 1965. 164 pp. $5.00.

These annotated translations of Cherokee charms and magic formulas are accompanied by a discussion of their words, images, background, and purpose.

KIMBALL, YEFFE, Osage

The Art of American Indian Cooking, co-authored by Jean Anderson. Garden City, New York: Doubleday and Co., Inc., 1965. 215 pp. Illus. $5.50. Also paperbound: New York: Avon Books, $.95.

American Indian recipes adapted for today's kitchen include information about foods and food habits of American Indians.

KING, CHERYL MILLS (WAH-BE-GWO-NESE), Chippewa

Ojibway Indian Legends. Marquette, Michigan: Northern Michigan Univ. Press, 1972. 20 pp. Illus. $2.95.

The author presents her renderings of two legends told by Ojibway (Chippewa) Indians to Henry R. Schoolcraft and also includes an explanation of the importance of fasting as part of Indian religion.

KLAH, HASTEEN, Navajo

Myth of Mountain Chant, recorded and retold in shorter form by Mary C. Wheelwright. Bulletin No. 5. Santa Fe, New Mexico: Museum of Navajo Ceremonial Art, Inc., 1951. pp. 1-6. Out of print.

This myth is about the son of Bear Woman, his childhood adventures, and the ceremonies he learned from Navajo gods.

Navajo Creation Myth: The Story of the Emergence, recorded by Mary C. Wheelwright. Navajo Religion Series Vol. 1. Santa Fe, New Mexico: Museum of Navajo Ceremonial Art, Inc., 1942. 237 pp. Illus. Out of print.

A general introduction about Navajo myths, ceremonies, sandpaintings and their rituals accompanies the Navajo creation myth, songs based on the myth, material on the Blessing Chant, and sandpaintings from the Blessing Chant. A glossary from the creation myth is included.

Tleji or Yehbechai Myth, retold in shorter form by Mary C. Wheelwright. Bulletin No. 1. Santa Fe, New Mexico: Museum of Navajo Ceremonial Art, Inc., 1938. 12 pp. Out of print.

This myth about a young Navajo boy named the Dreamer involves his adventures among Navajo Gods who teach him certain ceremonies that he must in turn teach to "Earth" people when he returns to them.

Wind Chant, recorded and retold in shorter form by Mary C. Wheelwright. Bulletin No. 4. Santa Fe, New Mexico: Museum of Navajo Ceremonial Art, Inc., 1946. pp. 1-6. Out of print.

This myth is about a Navajo boy turned into a snake and the healing ceremonies conducted by the Wind People in curing him.

KUNI; PAUL; BLIND TOM, *et al.,* Walapai
Walapai Ethnology, ed. by A. L. Kroeber. Memoirs of the American Anthropological Association No. 42. Menasha, Wisconsin: American Anthropological Association, 1935. pp. 205-229. Out of print.

Four brief autobiographies reveal various facets of the culture of the Walapai in the Southwest during the last quarter of the nineteenth century and the first quarter of the twentieth. Information is included on the acculturation process as the Walapai see it.

LADUKE, VINCENT (SUN BEAR), Chippewa
At Home in the Wilderness. Healdsburg, California: Naturegraph Publishers, 1969. 90 pp. Illus. $3.00.

This book by a Chippewa discusses survival in the outdoors. Chapters cover vegetable and fruit growing, use of wild plants and herbs, hunting, firemaking, soap making, blazing trails, and making shelters.

Buffalo Hearts. Healdsburg, California: Naturegraph Publishers, 1970. 128 pp. Illus. $6.00. Also paperbound: $3.00.

The author presents a general account of the philosophy, legends, culture, and history of Indians, including a dozen or more brief sketches of great Indian heroes.

LaFLESCHE, FRANCIS, Omaha
The Middle Five: Indian Schoolboys of the Omaha Tribe. Madison: Univ. of Wisconsin Press, 1963. 152 pp. Illus. $2.50 paperbound.

This reprint of a 1900 edition describes LaFlesche's experiences at the Presbyterian Mission School, Bellevue, Nebraska, during the 1860's.

The Omaha Tribe, co-authored by Alice Cunningham Fletcher. Lincoln: Univ. of Nebraska Press, 1972. 660 pp. Illus. 2 vols. $7.00 paperbound. $3.50 each.

The authors discuss the political, social, and economic organization as well as the customs, ceremonies, language and beliefs of the Omaha Tribe in the nineteenth century, before and after contact with whites. This is a reprint of the U. S. Bureau of American Ethnology, Twenty-seventh Annual Report, 1911. Also available: Johnson Reprint Corp., $27.50.

The Osage Tribe: Rite of the Chiefs; Sayings of the Ancient Men. New York: Johnson Reprint Corp. 592 pp. Illus. $20.00.

Two ancient Osage rites reflecting tribal law and religion are given in Osage with both literal and free English translations. This is a reprint of the U. S. Bureau of American Ethnology, Thirty-sixth Annual Report, 1921.

The War Ceremony and Peace Ceremony of the Osage Indians. U. S. Bureau of American Ethnology, Bulletin 101. Washington: Government Printing Office, 1939. 280 pp. Out of print.

Songs and rituals are presented in English and Osage.

Who Was the Medicine Man? 32nd Annual Report of Fairmont Park Art Association. Hampton, Virginia: Hampton Institute Press, 1905. 13 pp. Illus. Out of print.

In this speech, LaFlesche discusses the role of the medicine man in Indian life.

LAME DEER, CHIEF JOHN (FIRE), Sioux
Lame Deer: Seeker of Visions, and Richard Erdoes. New York: Simon and Schuster, Inc., 1972. 288 pp. Illus. $7.95. Also paperbound: $2.95.

Lame Deer, a Sioux medicine man born in 1903 in South Dakota, gives a highly imaginative account of his life. He describes conditions on the Rosebud Sioux Reservation and discusses aspects of modern Sioux religion.

LaPOINTE, FRANK, Sioux

The Sioux Today. New York: The Macmillan Company, 1972. 144 pp. Illus. $4.95.

In these vignettes of the lives of 24 Sioux young men and women today, the author unfolds the stories of such people as Chuck, who decides to let his hair grow and is called a "militant," Louis, who does not want to admit to being a Sioux; Shirley, who at fourteen serves as mother to five brothers and sisters; and Betty, a "new Indian" who refuses to be called a "squaw."

LaPOINTE, JAMES, Sioux

Legends of the Lakota. San Francisco, California: The Indian Historian Press, 1974. $7.00. Also paperbound: $4.00.

James LaPointe, a 78-year-old man, has translated the stories he heard from elders of his tribe about life and death, earth and air, mountains and rivers of his Dakota country.

LEFT HANDED, Navajo

Son of Old Man Hat: A Navajo Autobiography, as told to Walter Dyk. Lincoln: Univ. of Nebraska Press, 1967. 378 pp. $4.50. Also paperbound: $2.25.

In this reprint of a 1938 edition, an old man recalls his first twenty years. Through an interpreter, he deals with such subjects as Navajo sex mores, family relationships, customs, and philosophy of life.

LION, NEWELL, Penobscot

Penobscot Transformer Tales, ed. by Frank G. Speck. New York: Kraus Reprint Co., pp. 187-244. $16.00 paperbound.

Lion's version of the transformer-trickster cycle in Penobscot, a tribe located in Maine, and translated texts with a brief introduction by Speck are included. This is a reprint of International Journal of American Linguistics, Vol. I, No. 3, 1918.

LONE DOG, LOUISE, Mohawk-Delaware

Strange Journey: The Vision Quest of a Psychic Indian Woman. Healdsburg, California: Naturegraph Publishers, 1964. $1.50 paperbound.

A psychic woman records her visions.

LONG, JAMES LARPENTEUR (FIRST BOY),
Assiniboine
The Assiniboines: From the Accounts of the Old Ones Told to First Boy, ed. and with an introduction by Michael Stephen Kennedy. Norman: Univ. of Oklahoma Press, 1961. 209 pp. Illus. Out of print.

Long interviewed and recorded twenty-five of the oldest members of the Assiniboine Tribe living in the 1930's. Their facts, stories, and recollections tell of the Assiniboine way of life.

LONG LANCE, CHIEF BUFFALO CHILD, Croatan
Long Lance. New York: Cosmopolitan Book Corp., 1928. 278 pp. Illus. Out of print.

The author describes the experiences of the last tribes to encounter the advancing white man in the far Northwest (northern Montana, Alberta, Saskatchewan, and British Columbia) during the last quarter of the nineteenth century and the beginning of the twentieth.

Redman Echoes: Comprising the Writings of Chief Buffalo Child Long Lance and Biographical Sketches by His Friends. Los Angeles: Frank Wiggins Trade School, Dept. of Printing, 1933. 219 pp. Out of print.

The author describes tribes of the Northwest and western Canada during the late nineteenth and early twentieth centuries. He includes poetry, stories about Carlisle and West Point, and descriptions of tribal customs and ceremonies.

LOPEZ, RAFAEL, Yaqui, see CASTRO, AMBROSIO.

LORENSO, Isleta Pueblo
Pueblo Indian Folk-Stories, as told to Charles F. Lummis. New York: The Century Co., 1910. 257 pp. Illus. Out of print.

Thirty-one Isleta Pueblo folk-stories reflect the beliefs, history, and customs of this people, located in New Mexico.

LOWRY, ANNIE, Paiute
Karnee: A Paiute Narrative, ed. by Lalla Scott. Reno: Univ. of Nevada Press, 1966. 149 pp. $5.25. Also paperbound: Greenwich, Connecticut: Fawcett Publications, Inc., $.95.

A Paiute woman who was born about 1860 in Nevada narrates her life story, including a biography of her mother, Sau-tau-nee. Paiute history, legends, beliefs and customs before and after contact with white men are discussed.

MACK, CHARLIE, Ute, see TILLOHASH, TONY

MANUEL, GEORGE, Shuswap
The Fourth World: An Indian Reality and Social Change. Don Mills, Ontario: Collier-Macmillan of Canada, Ltd., 1973. About 300 pp. Illus. $7.00. Also paperbound: $3.00.

MARIA, CASA and **PESITA, JUAN,** Apache
Jicarilla Apache Texts, ed. by Pliny Earle Goddard. Anthropological Papers of the American Museum of Natural History Vol. VIII. New York: The Trustees, 1911. pp. 1-276. Out of print.

Myths, tales, traditions, personal experiences, ceremonies and other information concerning cultural ways of Apaches are presented in Apache and English texts.

MARKOOSIE, Eskimo
Harpoon of the Hunter. Montreal: McGill-Queen's Univ. Press, 1970. 81 pp. Illus. $4.95.

The hero of this story, young Kamik, tracks down a wounded polar bear and makes a long journey home alone after his companions have been killed. Life in the Canadian Arctic is depicted as an unrelenting, brutal, often fatal, struggle for survival. Illustrations are by Germaine Arnaktauyok.

MATHEWS, JOHN JOSEPH, Osage
Life and Death of an Oilman: The Career of E. W. Marland. Norman: Univ. of Oklahoma Press, 1952. 259 pp. Illus. Out of print.

This biography of Marland (1874-1941) gives an account of his famous Oklahoma oil strikes and his dealings in high finance.

The Osages: Children of the Middle Waters. Norman: Univ. of Oklahoma Press, 1961. 826 pp. Illus. $12.50.

This history of the Osage Tribe covers the periods before and after the coming of Europeans.

Sundown. New York: Longmans, Green, and Co., 1934. 312 pp. Out of print.

This is a novel about Chal Windzer, born about the turn of the century on the Osage Reservation in Oklahoma. Windzer goes to college, trains and serves as an aviator, and eventually returns to his own people after oil has been discovered on tribal lands. The changes in Osage life and the destructive role of alien ideals and customs in Osage culture are treated.

Talking to the Moon. Chicago: Univ. of Chicago Press, 1945. 243 pp. Out of print.

Mathews presents the Osage interpretation for each of the twelve appearances of the moon, and the special significance for the earth of each appearance.

Wah'Kon-Tah: The Osage and the White Man's Road. Norman: Univ. of Oklahoma Press, 1932, 1968. 359 pp. Illus. $5.95.

A journal kept by Major Laban J. Miles, the government agent to the Osages in Oklahoma from 1878 to 1931, provides the basis for this narrative. Mr. Mathews interprets the journal in light of his intimate knowledge of the tribe.

MAUNGWUDAUS, Chippewa
Remarks Concerning the Ojibway Indians, By One of Themselves—Called Maungwudaus. Leeds, England: C. A. Wilson and Co., 1847. 12 pp. Out of print.

The author lists the members of a party of Chippewas visiting England, France, Belgium, Ireland and Scotland in 1846-1847 and gives some brief facts concerning Chippewa religion. Testimonials presented to the visitors are included.

MAYOKOK, ROBERT, Eskimo
Mr. Mayokok, a well-known artist, has written and illustrated five paperbound booklets:

The Alaskan Eskimo (11 pp.) contains information on Eskimo food, native clothing, hunting and fishing. $.50.

Eskimo Customs (36 pp.) tells of such customs as piercing lips and tattooing and also has information on the Eskimo language. $1.50.

Eskimo Life (21 pp.) tells about oogrook, hunting, catching birds and arctic hare. $1.50.

Eskimo Stories (42 pp.) is a selection of traditional stories. $1.50.

True Eskimo Stories (36 pp.) tells about the hair seal, seal hunting, how the seal is used, dog teams, walrus and driftwood. $1.00.

Order from: Mr. Robert Mayokok, 1406 Twining Avenue, Anchorage, Alaska 99504. (Payment must accompany order.)

McGAA, ED, Sioux
Red Cloud: The Story of an American Indian. Minneapolis: Dillon Press, 1971. 54 pp. Illus. $3.95.

Red Cloud, an Oglala Sioux, struggled during the second half of the nineteenth century to save his people from cultural and physical destruction. This great leader emerges as a vigorous man whose incisive mind enables him to state his case with sharp wit and sly humor. Written by a member of the Oglala Sioux Tribe, this biography contains information about Sioux culture.

McGREGOR, WALTER, Haida, see STEVENS, TOM.

McGUFF, PETE, Wishram, see SIMPSON, LOUIS.

McLAUGHLIN, MARIE L., Sioux

Myths and Legends of the Sioux. Bismarck, North Dakota: Bismarck Tribune Co., 1916. 200 pp. Illus. Out of print.

Thirty-eight myths and legends told to Mrs. McLaughlin by older men and women of the Sioux Tribe deal with "simple things and creatures of the great out-of-doors and the epics of their doings." A short autobiography is included.

McNICKLE, D'ARCY, Flathead

Indian Man: A Life of Oliver LaFarge. Bloomington: Indiana Univ. Press, 1971. 288 pp. Illus. $7.95.

Mr. McNickle's biography follows Mr. LaFarge from his boyhood through his years at Groton and Harvard where he first became a member of summer archeological expeditions among Indian tribes, his coming to maturity as a writer and Mayan scholar, his World War II experience and his years as president of the Association on American Indian Affairs, Inc.

The Indian Tribes of the United States: Ethnic and Cultural Survival. New York: Oxford Univ. Press, Inc., 1962. 79 pp. $2.25 paperbound.

Indian attempts to adjust to Anglo-American culture in contemporary American society are the subject of this work. This book is being thoroughly revised and greatly expanded for a 1974 republication. The tentative title, *North American Tribalism*, will cost approximately $5.00 hardbound and $1.95 paperbound.

Indians and Other Americans, with Harold E. Fey. New York: Harper and Row, Publishers, 1970. 274 pp. Illus. $1.25 paperbound.

This comprehensive survey reviews the contacts between Indian and European colonists, wars, treaties, land deals, educative attempts, effects of relocation, urbanization, industrialization, and contemporary self-help programs designed to help Indians retain dignity and a sense of identity.

Runner in the Sun: A Story of Indian Maize. New York: Holt, Rinehart and Winston, 1954. 234 pp. Illus. $3.27.

An adventure story as well as the history of a town settled centuries before Columbus set sail from Spain, this novel is a scholarly reconstruction of the life, customs and beliefs of the ancient cliff-dwelling settlements of the southwestern United States. Salt, a teenage boy, is chosen to make a hazardous journey to Mexico in search of a hardier strain of corn and a better life for the people of his village. Illustrations are by Allan Houser.

The Surrounded. New York: Dodd, Mead, and Co., 1936. 297 pp. Out of print.

This novel about a tribe living on a reservation in western Montana focuses on the conflict between a boy's desire for a wider life and the traditions of his tribe.

They Came Here First: The Epic of the American Indian. Philadelphia: J. B. Lippincott Co., 1949. 352 pp. Out of print.

Mr. McNickle traces the history of American Indians, from the first migrations to North America to their near-extinction under white domination.

MITCHELL, EMERSON BLACKHORSE, Navajo
Miracle Hill: The Story of a Navajo Boy, with T. D. Allen. Norman: Univ. of Oklahoma Press, 1967. 230 pp. $5.95.

This is an autobiographical account of a young Navajo's life, from his birth in a hogan to his coming of age, from his relationships with his own family and environment to his dealings with the world of the white man.

MITCHELL, FRANK, Navajo, see CURLY, SLIM.

MITCHELL, WAYNE, Penobscot, see THOMPSON, JEAN.

MOCKINGBIRD, JON, Apache
The Wokosani Road: A Novel of Indian Lore in the Southwest. New York: Exposition Press, 1963. 381 pp. Out of print.

This novel, set in the Pacific during World War II and in the Southwest after the war, contains information about legends, traditions, and the religion of Indians of the lower Mississippi and the Southwest.

MOISES, ROSALIO, Yaqui

The Tall Candle: The Personal Chronicle of a Yaqui Indian, with Jane Holden and William Curry Holden. Lincoln: Univ. of Nebraska Press, 1971. 251 pp. $7.50.

Moisés, born in 1896 in Sonora, Mexico, gives a narrative account of his life in northwestern Mexico and Arizona until 1951, when Moisés leaves hunger and tragedy behind in the Yaqui Valley and moves to Texas. He includes material on the history of the Yaqui Tribe.

MOMADAY, N. SCOTT, Kiowa

House Made of Dawn. New York: Harper and Row, 1969. 224 pp. $4.95. Also paperbound: New York: New American Library. $0.95.

This novel is about an ex-serviceman's relationship to two worlds—Indian and non-Indian—after World War II. He finds it difficult to fit into the white man's world or to go home to his Pueblo. Pulitzer Prize winner.

The Names. New York: Harper and Row, Publishers. Illus. 1974.

This is a family chronicle about the author's Indian forebears and his own life.

The Way to Rainy Mountain. Albuquerque: Univ. of New Mexico Press, 1969. 89 pp. Illus. by A. M. Momaday. $4.95. Also paperbound: New York: Ballantine Books. $1.25.

Mr. Momaday retells the story of the migration of the Kiowas from the headwaters of the Yellowstone River in what is now western Montana to Rainy Mountain in the Southern Plains. The journey, begun three hundred years ago, is recalled in three voices: legendary, historical, and contemporary.

MOMADAY, NATACHEE SCOTT, Cherokee, ed.

American Indian Authors. Boston: Houghton Mifflin Co., 1972. 151 pp. $2.20 paperbound.

This book contains 26 examples of the works of American Indian authors. Three types of work are included: the oral literature of Indians in the form of legends, chants, prayers and poems; historical and biographical recordings of those Indians who told their stories to others through interpreters, and the fiction, nonfiction and poetry of 20th century Indians who have adopted the English language as a form of communication.

MONTURE, ETHEL BRANT, Mohawk

Famous Indians: Brant, Crowfoot, and Oronhyatekha. Toronto: Clarke, Irwin, and Co., Ltd., 1960. 160 pp. Illus. $3.50.

In this volume are the life stories of Brant (Mohawk), Crowfoot (Blackfeet) and Oronhyatekha or Peter Martin (Mohawk).

Joseph Brant, Mohawk, with Harvey Chalmers. East Lansing, Michigan: Michigan State Univ. Press, 1955. 364 pp. Out of print.

This biography of Brant, an eighteenth-century Mohawk, was written by one of his descendants.

West to the Setting Sun, with Harvey Chalmers. New York: The Macmillan Co., 1943. 362 pp. Out of print.

The career of Joseph Brant, in a book combining factual biography and historical fiction, is treated against a background of military action. A picture emerges of a people struggling to preserve their traditions and physical surroundings.

MORGAN, WILLIAM, Navajo

Human-Wolves Among the Navajo. Yale Univ. Publications in Anthropology, No. 11. New Haven: Yale Univ. Press, 1936. 43 pp. Out of print.

The author discusses the Navajo belief in human-wolves, men and women disguised in wolf or mountain-lion skin who practice witchcraft. He treats the human-wolves as a variable in Navajo culture as a whole and tells the stories of several Navajos who share this belief.

Navajo Historical Selections, co-authored by Robert W. Young. Lawrence, Kansas: Bureau of Indian Affairs, 1954. 209 pp. $1.00 paperbound. Available from Publications Service, Haskell Institute, Lawrence, Kansas 66044.

These stories and articles, written by Navajos, record events from the past and also give Navajo attitudes and reactions to historic events. Navajo and English texts are provided.

MORRISEAU, NORVAL, Chippewa

Legends of My People: The Great Ojibway, ed. by Selwyn Dewdney. Scarborough, Ontario: McGraw Hill Co. of Canada, Ltd., 1965. 130 pp. Illus. by $6.75.

This collection of the beliefs, tales, and legends of the Ojibway (Chippewa) of Lake Nipigon and the Thunder Bay district (Ontario) is accompanied by the author's paintings. The introduction includes a biography of Morriseau and some history of the Chippewas in Canada. The first chapter contains an autobiographical sketch.

MOUNTAIN WOLF WOMAN, Winnebago

Mountain Wolf Woman, Sister of Crashing Thunder: The Autobiography of a Winnebago Woman, ed. by Nancy Oestreich Lurie. Ann Arbor: Univ. of Michigan Press, 1961. 142 pp. $4.95. Also paperbound: $1.95.

Mountain Wolf Woman, 75 years of age, records everyday events of her long life. This book contains information about Winnebago culture in Wisconsin and Nebraska.

MR. MOUSTACHE, Navajo

A Navajo Personal Document with a Brief Paretian Analysis, ed. by Clyde Kluckhohn, Southwestern Journal of Anthropology, Vol. I. Albuquerque: Univ. of New Mexico Press, 1945. pp. 260-283. Out of print.

This brief life story of a Navajo born in 1868, told to Kluckhohn through an interpreter, reveals ways in which social conditioning is carried on within the Tribe and contains data on the values of Navajo society.

MURIE, JAMES R., Pawnee

Pawnee Indian Societies. Anthropological Papers of the American Museum of Natural History, Vol. XI, Part VII. New York: The Trustees, 1914. pp. 543-644. Out of print.

Discussions of Pawnee societies and a general outline of the tribal ceremonial scheme are accompanied by descriptions of the place and significance of the societies in Pawnee culture.

Traditions of the Skidi Pawnee, with George Amos Dorsey. Memoirs of the American Folklore Society, Vol. VIII. Boston: Houghton Mifflin and Co., 1904. 366 pp. Out of print.

Pawnee tales about tribal origins, rituals, medicine men, and encounters with animals are grouped here to convey the culture of the Pawnees.

NATIONAL INDIAN BROTHERHOOD
Suite 1610, Varette Building
130 Albert Street
Ontario, K1P 5G4 Canada

The NIB is currently preparing a series of pamphlets concerning the Indian peoples in Canada. Some of these pamphlets are available: *Indian Control of Indian Education; Historical Development of Aboriginal Political Associations in Canada; Documentation,* and *Reference Aids—Bibliographies: Vols. 1, 2, 3* (bibliographies of periodic literature concerning contemporary Canadian Indian affairs). Others still at the printers are *Canada and the Environment* and *Aboriginal People, a Selected Bibliography.* Write for information.

NEPTUNE, FRANCOIS, Wawenock
Wawenock Myth Texts from Maine, ed. by Frank G. Speck. U. S. Bureau of American Ethnology Forty-third Annual Report. Washington: Government Printing Office, 1928. pp. 169-197. Out of print.

Five myths in Wawenock text and a free English translation are accompanied by an introduction giving a brief history of this Maine tribe.

NEPTUNE, MARTIN, Penobscot, see THOMPSON, JEAN.

NEPTUNE, NOEL, Penobscot, see JOSEPHS, TOMAH.

NEQUATEWA, EDMUND, Hopi
Truth of a Hopi: Stories Relating to the Origin, Myths, and Clan Histories of the Hopi. Museum of Northern Arizona, Bulletin No. 8. Flagstaff, Arizona: Northland Press, 1967. 136 pp. $4.95.

This reprint of a 1936 edition contains stories from Hopi tradition, myth, and history. The sacred beliefs, wanderings, and trials of a group of Hopi clans are also recounted.

NEWELL, WILLIAM B., Mohawk
Crime and Justice Among the Iroquois. Montreal: Caughnawaga Historical Society, 1965. 92 pp. Out of print.

Iroquois society is briefly described here, with an analysis of social life, the relationship of crime to the society, specific crimes, punishments, and laws.

NEWLAND, SAM and STEWART, JACK, Paiute

Two Paiute Autobiographies, as told to Julian Haynes Steward. New York: Kraus Reprint Co. pp. 423-438. $25.00.

Two men, each nearly 100 years old but widely divergent in personality, tell the stories of their lives and give insights into the dynamic aspects of Paiute culture. Both men reached maturity before the coming of the white man to eastern California in 1861. This is a reprint of Univ. of California Publications in American Archaeology and Ethnology, Vol. 33, No. 5, 1934.

NEZ PERCE TRIBE

Ne Mee Poom Tit Wah Tit (Nez Perce Legends). Lapwai, Idaho: Nez Perce Tribe, 1972. 214 pp. Illus. $12.50 plus $.50 handling. Available from Nez Perce Tribe, Box 305, Lapwai, Idaho 83540.

Coyote, the principal character in these legends, is known as a trickster-transformer. Sometimes a man, sometimes an animal, he possesses supernatural powers and can change himself, other animals, people and objects in various ways. He is a silly, clumsy, stupid, laughable rascal who gets into one scrape after another but he is also a cheerful, happy creature who is in no way evil. By acting out man's socially disruptive drives, the trickster (Coyote) reveals in these stories the results of violating conventional Nez Perce mores. Stories of Coyote's exploits are used to teach Nez Perce children how to behave properly and to instill in a child values which will help him become a good person. This book, sponsored and edited by the Nez Perce Tribe, is the first of a three-phase project on the history and culture of the Nez Perce Tribe.

NIATUM, DUANE, Klallam

After the Death of an Elder Klallam and Other Poems. Phoenix: The Baleen Press, 1970. 64 pp. Illus. $6.00. Also paperbound: $2.40. Available from: Baleen Press, P. O. Box 13448, Phoenix, Arizona 85002.

This collection of 32 poems by a poet from the Northwest Coast is illustrated with adaptations of Northwest Coast Indian art by Navajo artist, Mary Morez.

Ascending Red Cedar Moon. New York: Harper and Row, Publishers, 1974.

The author's fourth volume of verse, here is the first full length collection by this young Klallam poet, now living in New York.

A Cycle for Woman in the Field. Baltimore: Laughing Man Press, 1973. 15 pp. Illus. $1.00 paperbound. Available from: Laughing Man Press, 2501 Queen Ann Road, Baltimore, Maryland 21216.

This book contains a series of love poems.

Taos Pueblo. Saratoga Springs: Greenfield Review Press, 1973. 25 pp. Illus. $1.25 paperbound. Available from: Greenfield Review Press, Greenfield Center, Saratoga Springs, New York 12833.

Of the five poems in this booklet, the first is a lengthy one concerning the Taos Pueblo, one of the oldest pueblos in the Southwest. Cover drawings and illustrations are by Wendy Rose, a Pueblo Indian.

NICOLAR, JOSEPH, Penobscot

The Life and Traditions of the Red Man. Bangor, Maine: C. H. Glass and Co., Printers, 1893. 147 pp. Out of print.

This traditional Penobscot story about the works and teaching of Klose-kur-beḥ, the first person to come upon the earth, is intended "to show the simple and natural state of life, habits, and ways as they existed" among Indians.

NOWELL, CHARLES JAMES, Kwakiutl

Smoke from Their Fires: The Life of a Kwakiutl Chief, ed. by Chellan Stearns Ford. Hamden, Connecticut: Archon, 1968. 248 pp. Illus. $6.50.

Nowell, born in 1870, tells the story of his life and comments on Kwakiutl society before and after contacts with whites. This is a reprint of the 1940 edition.

NULIGAK, Eskimo

I, Nuligak. Translated from the Eskimo by Maurice Metayer. Toronto: Peter Martin Associates, Inc. 1968. 208 pp. $5.95. Also paperbound: New York: Pocket Books, $1.25.

This autobiography of a member of the Kitigariukmeut tribe of Canadian Eskimos spans the years from 1895 to 1966. It is simply told and reveals the gaiety, laughter and warmth of Eskimo community life as well as the physical hardship and privations of life in the harsh Arctic environment.

OCCOM, SAMSON, Mohegan

A Sermon at the Execution of Moses Paul, An Indian. New Haven, Connecticut: T. and S. Green, 1772. 32 pp. Out of print.

Reverend Occom, one of the first Indians to study at Dartmouth College, preaches a sermon full of Christian theology at the desire of Moses Paul who was executed on September 2, 1772, for murder.

OCCOM, SAMSON, Mohegan, see ASHPO, SAMUEL.

OKAKOK, GUY, Eskimo

Okakok's Alaska. Fairbanks, Alaska: P.E.O. Sisterhood, 1959. 31 pp. Illus. Out of print.

This booklet contains selections from "Pt. Barrow News," a column written by Okakok for the *Fairbanks Daily News-Miner.* The items in the booklet reflect the newsworthy events of Point Barrow, Alaska, from 1955-1959.

OLD MAN BUFFALO GRASS, Navajo

The Dine: Origin Myths of the Navajo Indians, ed. by Aileen O'Bryan. U. S. Bureau of American Ethnology, Bulletin 163. Washington: Government Printing Office, 1956. 187 pp. Illus. Out of print.

This collection of origin myths includes: The Creation, or Age of Beginning; The Order of Things; The Age of the Gods, or the Story of the Twins; and The Wanderings, or Age of the Patriarchs.

OLD MEXICAN, Navajo

Old Mexican: A Navajo Autobiography, as told to Walter Dyk. New York: Johnson Reprint Corp. 218 pp. $10.00 paperbound.

This narrative of Old Mexican's life from 1871 (when he was five) to 1919 is mainly about adult life in Navajo society. This is a reprint of Viking Fund Publications in Anthropology, No. 8, 1947.

OLEDOSKA, Abenaki, see PARKER, CHIEF EVERETT.

OQUILLUK, WILLIAM, Eskimo
People of Kauwerak: Legendary History of the Northern Eskimo. Anchorage, Alaska: Alaska Methodist Univ. Press, 1972. About 245 pp. Illus. $7.50. Also paperbound: $5.00.

The author, born in 1896 at Point Hope, Alaska, writes the history and legends of the Eskimo people of the Seward Peninsula based on the stories told to him by several elderly Eskimo people. Photographs illustrate the region where different historical events took place.

ORTIZ, ALFONSO, San Juan Pueblo
Project Head Start in an Indian Community. 70 pp. $3.29. $.65 microfiche card. Available from: ERIC Document Reproduction Service, NCR Co., 4936 Fairmont Ave., Bethesda, Maryland 20014. Use the book's reference number, ED 014 329.

Dr. Ortiz, a Tewa from San Juan Pueblo in New Mexico, discusses the influence of historical, social, and cultural factors upon the early learning processes of San Juan Pueblo Indian children as related to the conduct of Head Start Programs.

"Ritual Drama and the Pueblo World View," in *New Perspectives on the Pueblos,* ed. by Alfonso Ortiz. Albuquerque: Univ. of New Mexico Press, 1972. 340 pp. Illus. $11.00.

In this essay, Ortiz discusses the generalized Pueblo world view with an emphasis on space and a different view of time, illustrating some aspects of this view by focusing attention on calendric ritual dramas which are universal in the Pueblos. Particular attention is paid to recurrent themes concerned with space and time, burlesque, caricature, mock violence, formality, gluttony, licensed obscenity, and age, status, and sex reversals.

The Tewa World: Space, Time, Being, and Becoming in a Pueblo Society. Chicago: Univ. of Chicago Press, 1969. $8.00. Also paperbound: $2.45.

This analysis of the complex cosmological and ritual systems of the Tewa, an eastern Pueblo society of the Southwest, is one of the most complete descriptions and interpretations ever published on the world view of an Indian tribe.

To Carry Forth the Vine: An Anthology of Native North American Poetry, with Margaret D. Ortiz. New York: Columbia Univ. Press, 1974.

This collection of American Indian and Eskimo traditional oral literature, from ancient times to the present, includes prayers, songs, short myths, and stories drawn from North and South America.

OSKISON, JOHN MILTON, Cherokee
Brothers Three. New York: The Macmillan Co., 1935. 448 pp. Out of print.

This novel, which starts in 1873, tells the story of an Oklahoma farm and the family that owned it.

A Texas Titan: The Story of Sam Houston. Garden City, New York: Doubleday, Doran and Co., Inc. 1929. 311 pp. Out of print.

This story of Sam Houston's life includes his numerous contacts and friendships with Indians.

Tecumseh and His Times: The Story of a Great Indian. New York: G. P. Putnam's Sons, 1938. 244 pp. Out of print.

This is a biography of Tecumseh, a Shawnee, who struggled valiantly to protect Indian lands from white encroachment.

OWENS, NARCISSA, Cherokee
Memoirs of Narcissa Owens. Washington: ?, 1907. 126 pp. Illus. Out of print.

These recollections of a Cherokee woman, born in 1831, include stories of her ancestors and their ancient traditions, and of her early life, marriage, and teaching until 1907.

OWL, MRS. SAMSON; BROWN, MARGARET WILEY; GORDON, SALLY, *et al.,* Cherokee
Catawba Texts, ed. by Frank G. Speck. New York: AMS Press, Inc., $7.50.

Catawba tales narrated by Mrs. Owl and several other members of the tribe through an interpreter are presented in Catawba and English texts (southeastern United States). This is a reprint of Columbia Univ. Contributions to Anthropology Vol. XXIV, 1934.

PARKER, ARTHUR CASWELL, Seneca
A History of the Seneca Indians. Empire State Historical Publication No. 43. Port Washington, New York: Ira J. Friedman, Inc., 1967. 162 pp. $7.50.

Originally published in 1926, this book details the history and culture of the Senecas from their beginnings through the first quarter of the twentieth century.

The Indian How Book. Garden City, New York: Doubleday, Doran and Co., 1937. 355 pp. Out of print.

This book focuses on life in camp and on the trail.

The Life of General Ely S. Parker: Last Grand Sachem of the Iroquois and General Grant's Military Secretary. Buffalo Historical Society Publications Vol. 23. Buffalo, New York: Buffalo Historical Society, 1919. 346 pp. Out of print.

Told by his great-nephew, this narrative of the life of E. S. Parker, who was born in 1828, includes material on the home life, social status, and relationships of a Seneca family.

Parker on the Iroquois. Syracuse, New York: Syracuse Univ. Press, 1968. 472 pp. Illus. $8.95.

A compilation of early twentieth century works, this book includes "Iroquois Uses of Maize and Other Food Plants," "The Code of Handsome Lake, the Seneca Prophet," and "The Constitution of the Five Nations."

Red Jacket: Last of the Senecas. New York: McGraw-Hill Book Co., 1952. 288 pp. Illus. Out of print.

This history of Red Jacket, a Seneca born in 1750, includes narrative material expressing his preference for the Seneca way of life and details his efforts to protect the Senecas from the encroachments of an alien civilization.

Seneca Myths and Folk Tales. Buffalo Historical Society Publications Vol. 27. Buffalo: Buffalo Historical Society, 1923. 465 pp. Illus. Out of print.

This collection of oral literature from the Senecas of western New York State includes myths, legends, fiction, and traditions that reveal Seneca customs, interests, and daily life.

PARKER, CHIEF EVERETT, Seneca, and
OLEDOSKA, Abenaki
The Secret of No Face (An Ireokwa Epic). Santa Clara, California: Native American Publishing Co., 1972. 178 pp. Illus. $3.95 paperbound.

Parker, a Seneca from upstate New York, tells in this epic the myths and legends of the Cornhusk Doll—passing on the story to his Abenaki friend, Oledoska (Rising Sun). The stories in this book draw on the philosophy and moral teachings of Handsome Lake, a Seneca prophet who was a spiritual leader of his people in the early nineteenth century.

PARRISH, ESSIE, Kashaya, see JAMES, HERMAN.

PATENCIO, CHIEF FRANCISCO, Cahuilla
Desert Hours with Chief Patencio, as told to Kate Collins. Palm Springs: Palm Springs Desert Museum, 1971. 38 pp. Illus. $1.00 paperbound. Available from the Museum, 135 E. Tahquitz-McCallum Way, P. O. Box 2288, Palm Springs, California 92262.

In a series of dialogues, Patencio, whose words are exactly as they were recorded, gives historical information about the Cahuilla and other Indian tribes located in southern California.

Stories and Legends of the Palm Springs Indians, as told to Margaret Boynton. Palm Springs, California: Palm Springs Desert Museum, 1943. 132 pp. $2.00 paperbound. Available from the Museum, 135 E. Tahquitz-McCallum Way, P. O. Box 2288, Palm Springs, California 92262.

Chief Patencio narrates 15 legends and traditions of his California tribe to preserve them for his people. The second part of the book contains Patencio's story about his childhood and adult life in the late nineteenth and early twentieth centuries and includes information on local California history.

PAUL, Walapai, see KUNI.

PAYTIAMO, JAMES (FLAMING ARROW),
Acoma Pueblo
Flaming Arrow's People: By an Acoma Indian. New York: Duffield and Green, 1932. 158 pp. Illus. by Author. Out of print.

The author gives historical and cultural information about New Mexico's Acoma Pueblo.as he discusses his boyhood days.

PEEK, WILLIAM (METACOMET), Narragansett-Wampanoag, see SANDERS, THOMAS

PELLETIER, WILFRED, Odawa
"For every North American Indian who begins to disappear, I also begin to disappear," in *For Every North American Indian Who Begins to Disappear, I Also Begin to Disappear.* Toronto: Neewin Publishing Co., Ltd., 1971. pp. 3-23. $3.75 paperbound.

In this article, the author discusses Indian ways of experiencing the world and the ways in which they are in conflict with contemporary white society.

"Traditional Concepts of Organization," in *For Every North American Indian Who Begins to Disappear, I Also Begin to Disappear.* Toronto: Neewin Publishing Co., Ltd., 1971. pp. 79-85. $3.75 paperbound.

The author discusses the traditional Indian approach to organization and shows how it is not compatible with western European concepts of organization that have been introduced on Canadian Indian reserves.

Two Articles. Toronto: Neewin Publishing Co., Ltd. Unpaged. Illus. $1.25 paperbound.

In two articles, "Childhood in an Indian Village" (1969) and "Some Thoughts about Organization and Leadership" (1967), the author describes the attitudes and values he grew up with as a child in Canada and contrasts them with contemporary Canadian society's attitudes and values he has become familiar with since leaving his reservation community.

PESITA, JUAN, Apache, see MARIA, CASA.

PEYNETSA, ANDREW and **SANCHEZ, WALTER**, Zuni Pueblo
Finding the Center: Narrative Poetry of the Zuni Indians, translated by Dennis Tedlock. New York: Dial Press, 1972. 298 pp. $8.50. Also paperbound: $2.95.

The book contains a collection of "tales" regarded as fiction and "stories" regarded as historical truth translated from the spoken narratives of Peynetsa and Sanchez, both in their early sixties and living in New Mexico. Tedlock presents the poems with special notations guiding one in how to read them aloud. Notations indicate different lengths of breath, pauses, loudness or softness of specific words and phrases, syllable duration, speed and gesture. Tedlock's introduction discusses many aspects of Zuni narrative poetry.

PHINNEY, ARCHIE, Nez Perce
Nez Perce Texts. New York: AMS Press, Inc., $24.50.

This collection of ancient Nez Perce tales was narrated to the author by his sixty-year-old mother, Wayilatpu. Nez Perce and English texts are provided. This is a reprint of Columbia Univ. Contributions to Anthropology Vol. XXV, 1934.

PIERCE, CHIEF MARIS BRYANT, Seneca
Address on the Present Condition and Prospects of the Aboriginal Inhabitants of North America. Buffalo, New York: Steele's Press, 1838. 16 pp. Out of print.

Pierce argues that Indians have the capacity to learn and appreciate any of the principals of Christian civilization if they so desire. In the second part of the book Pierce tries to show that it would not improve the conditions of the Senecas to remove from New York to beyond the Mississippi River.

PIERRE, CHIEF GEORGE, Colville
American Indian Crisis. San Antonio, Texas: The Naylor Co., 1971. 216 pp. $8.95.

This discussion of contemporary Indian affairs by Pierre, who lives in Washington, includes information on the problems of Indians, a review of common solutions and explanations of his own recommendations. The author calls for a reexamination of the federal supervision structure, a revision of the Bureau of Indian Affairs, and vocational and personal counseling for young Indians.

Autumn's Bounty. San Antonio, Texas: The Naylor Co., 1972. 155 pp. $7.95.

This novel, set in modern-day Okanogan country (Washington), details the story of an old chief's hunt to track down a coyote that has killed a little girl and describes his efforts to prevent termination of federal services to his reservation.

PITCHLYNN, PETER PERKINS; FOLSOM, ISRAEL; and **GARLAND, SAMUEL,** *et al.,* Choctaw
Papers Relating to the Claims of the Choctaw Nation Against the United States Arising Under the Treaty of 1830. Washington: 1855. 53 pp. Out of print.

This book contains the letters written to President Franklin Pierce by the Choctaw delegation consisting of Pitchlynn, Israel Folsom, Samuel Garland, and Dickson W. Lewis. The writings concern the claims arising under the treaty of 1830, under which the Choctaws gave up their southern lands and moved to Oklahoma. Pitchlynn and his delegation discuss the non-fulfillment of treaty stipulations.

PITSEOLAK, Eskimo
Pitseolak: Pictures Out of My Life, from recorded interviews by Dorothy Eber. Seattle: Univ. of Washington Press, 1971. Unpaged. Illus. by author. $9.95.

Pitseolak, a well-known Eskimo artist, narrates her story of growing up in the Arctic, marrying, giving birth, living the old way and also the new. Pitseolak's story is also an account of Cape Dorset, Baffin Island, a Canadian Eskimo community. Some of the author's drawings in color and black-and-white are included as well as an Eskimo text of the story.

PLENTY-COUPS, Crow

Plenty-Coups, Chief of the Crows, ed. by Frank Bird Linderman. Lincoln: Univ. of Nebraska Press, 1962. 324 pp. $1.50 paperbound.

Eighty-year-old Chief Plenty-Coups discusses his boyhood, how he became chief, and how he participated in the tribal life of the Crow Indians. This book was originally published in 1930 as *American, The Life Story of a Great Indian, Plenty-Coups, Chief of the Crows.*

PLENTY-HAWK, Crow, see YELLOW BROW.

POKAGON, CHIEF SIMON, Potawatomi

O-Gî-Mäw-Kwĕ Mit-I-Gwä-Kî (Queen of the Woods). Hartford, Michigan: C. H. Engle, 1899. 255 pp. Out of print.

Out of a mixture of fact, fiction, and poetry, Pokagon, born in 1830, creates an historical novel centering about events in his life in the Great Lakes area. The book can also be read as a plea for racial justice and temperance. Also included are a biography of the author, a brief sketch of the Algonquin language, and an appendix of the author's public addresses.

The Red Man's Rebuke. Hartford, Michigan: C. H. Engle, 1893. 16 pp. Out of print.

This was originally printed on the bark of a white birch tree and presented at the World's Columbian Exposition in Chicago in 1893. In it, Pokagon gives an account of the betrayal of Indians since the advent of white men. Also known as *The Red Man's Greetings,* this pamphlet has been reprinted in "Pokagons," *Indiana Historical Society Publications,* Vol. 10, No. 5 (1933).

PORCUPINE DAY SCHOOL STUDENTS, Sioux

Photographs and Poems by Sioux Children. Rapid City, South Dakota: Tipi Shop, Inc., 1971. 80 pp. $2.50. Available from: Tipi Shop, Inc., P. O. Box 1270, Rapid City, South Dakota 57701.

Thirteen teenage students of the Porcupine Day School on the Pine Ridge Sioux Reservation in South Dakota took the photographs presented in this exhibition catalog. The pictures are accompanied by poems written by the student photographers and their classmates. The photographs explore many aspects of life and the natural environment of the Porcupine community and document western rural life during the winter season of 1969-1970. The poems are an extension of the photographic themes.

POSEY, ALEXANDER LAWRENCE, Creek
The Poems of Alexander Lawrence Posey, collected by Mrs. Minnie H. Posey. Topeka, Kansas: Crane and Co., Printers, 1910. 192 pp. Out of print.

This collection of poetry by Posey, born in 1873, deals either with some aspect of the natural environment or with some person. A biography of Posey is also included.

POT, BOB; COON, BILL; JAMES, BILL;
et al., Pomo
Pomo Indian Myths, ed. by Samuel Alfred Barrett and Ira Edwards. Public Museum of the City of Milwaukee, Bulletin, Vol. 15. Milwaukee, Wisconsin: Public Museum of the City of Milwaukee, 1933. 608 pp. Out of print, but available at $5.00 from The Museum of the American Indian, Broadway at 155th Street, New York, New York 10032.

This collection of Pomo myths includes stories of creation, supernatural beings, magic devices, tricksters, and animals. Included are an introduction discussing Pomo mythology and religious concepts and a large section of notes for all the myths. Also available: Johnson Reprint Corp., $25.00.

PRETTY SHIELD, Crow
Red Mother, ed. by Frank Bird Linderman. New York: John Day Co., 1932. 256 pp. Out of print.

In a conversation between Pretty Shield, a medicine woman of the Crow Tribe, born in the 1850's in Montana, and Linderman, Pretty Shield's childhood and early maturity are discussed. Some Crow myths, tales, and history are included.

PRINCE, ANNA; HOFFMAN, JOSEPH; VALOR, PALMER; *et al.,* Apache
Western Apache Raiding and Warfare, from notes of Grenville Goodwin; ed. by Keith H. Basso. Tucson: Univ. of Arizona Press, 1971. 330 pp. Illus. $5.95 paperbound.

The first part of this book contains chronologically arranged autobiographical narratives by six western Apaches covering events that occurred during the 1850's and 1860's. The narratives provide information about raiding, warfare, and Apache daily life. The second part contains briefer statements by western Apaches about specific aspects of weapons, war dances, leadership, taboos, scalping, and captives.

QOYAWAYMA, POLINGAYSI (ELIZABETH Q. WHITE), Hopi

No Turning Back: A True Account of a Hopi Indian Girl's Struggle to Bridge the Gap Between the World of Her People and the World of the White Man, as told to Vada F. Carlson. Albuquerque: Univ. of New Mexico Press, 1964. 180 pp. $5.95.

This is the autobiography of a Hopi woman, born about 1892, who chooses in her early youth to live in the white man's world. It includes information on Hopi legend, ceremony, religion, and philosophy.

RAY, CARL, Cree

Sacred Legends of the Sandy Lake Cree, ed. by James R. Stevens. Toronto: McClelland and Stewart, Ltd., 1971. 144 pp. Illus. by author. $6.95.

This is a collection of sacred legends of the Sandy Lake Cree (northwestern Ontario) as they have been told by the elder story-tellers. Stevens' introduction outlines the history of the Tribe and its way of life. A glossary of Cree terms is included.

RED HORSE OWNER, Sioux

Red Horse Owner's Winter Count: The Oglala Sioux 1786-1968, ed. by Joseph S. Karol. Martin, South Dakota: The Booster Publishing Co., 1969. 68 pp. Illus. $1.50 paperbound. Available from: Tipi Shop, Inc., P.O. Box 1270, Rapid City, South Dakota 57701.

The Sioux winter count is a calendric history and contains a yearly pictographic symbol (explained in the accompanying text) representing the people, places, or events that made each year notable.

RED JACKET, Seneca

A Long Lost Speech of Red Jacket, ed. by John Wentworth Sanborn. Friendship, New York: 1912. 6 pp. Out of print.

In this rare speech, delivered to the Rev. Elkanah Holmes in September 1803 at a council of the principal sachems of the New York Seneca, Onondaga and Cayuga nations, Red Jacket speaks in favor of building a house of worship also to be used for educating Seneca children. The reply of the Rev. Holmes is included. (Copy in the New York Public Library pamphlet collection.)

RED JACKET and FARMER'S BROTHER, Seneca

Indian Speeches: Delivered by Farmer's Brother and Red Jacket, Two Seneca Chiefs. Canandaigua, New York: James D. Bemis, 1809. 8 pp. Out of print.

This booklet contains a short introductory speech by Farmer's Brother given in November 1798 at a public council in upstate New York and a speech by Red Jacket given in the summer of 1805 at a Six Nations' Council, with a guest missionary attending. Red Jacket responds to the clergy's proposal to "enlighten the Indians' mind" by denouncing these efforts as a scheme to suppress the Indians' religion. (Also titled *Native Eloquence,* 1811.)

REDBIRD, DUKE, Chippewa

Red on White, by Marty Dunn. Toronto: New Press, 1971. Chicago: Follett Publishing Co., 1971. 121 pp. Illus. $6.95.

This biography of Duke Redbird contains extensive selections of his works. The poet, a 30-year-old Canadian Chippewa who was raised in white homes, has been at times a laborer, side-show freak, painter, poet, actor, writer, politician, and independent TV producer.

REDSKY, JAMES (ESQUEKESIK), Chippewa

Great Leader of the Ojibway: Mis-Quona-Queb, ed. by James R. Stevens. Toronto: McClelland and Stewart, Ltd., 1972. 127 pp. Illus. $7.95.

The author, a 73-year-old holy man, has written a collection of tales passed down from generation to generation about the Chippewa (Ojibway) war leader Mis-quonaqueb, a legendary hero of the Shoal Lake Chippewas (Manitoba, Canada) who probably lived in the area in the late 1700's-early 1800's. Descriptions of Chippewa religion and the society of medicine men are also provided by Redsky. Stevens includes a brief history of the tribe and a biography of Redsky.

REID, WILLIAM, Haida

Out of the Silence. New York: Harper and Row, 1972. 121 pp. Illus. $4.95 paperbound.

A collection of black-and-white photographs of Haida totem-pole carvings taken between 1966 and 1968 and poetic commentary by Reid, a Haida carver, evoke Northwest Coast Indian life and art.

RICKARD, CHIEF CLINTON, Tuscarora

Fighting Tuscarora: The Autobiography of Chief Clinton Rickard, ed. by Barbara Graymont. Syracuse: Syracuse Univ. Press, 1974. 224 pp. Illus. $10.50.

Chief Rickard, born in 1882, recalls his childhood poverty in the tribal world, his service with the army in the Philippines in the Spanish-American War, his brutal treatment in a Canadian jail, and his legal battles on behalf of his people with the U. S. government, New York State and Canada.

RIDDLE, JEFF., Modoc
The Indian History of the Modoc War. San Francisco: By the Author, 1914. 295 pp. Illus. Out of print.

The author, born in 1863 in California and son of a chief figure in the Modoc War of 1872-73, tells the Indian side of the story and presents information on Captain Jack's life and a vindication of his role in the war. He discusses the causes and history of the war up to the hanging of Captain Jack and other Modocs. Biographies of figures involved in this story as well as correspondence and official documents are included.

RIDGE, JOHN ROLLIN (YELLOW BIRD), Cherokee
The Life and Adventures of Joaquin Murieta, the Celebrated California Bandit. Norman: Univ. of Oklahoma Press, 1962. 159 pp. Illus. $2.95.

This romanticized biography of Murieta describes the life and career of California's most legendary bandit.

Poems. San Francisco: Henry Payot and Co., Publishers, 1868. 137 pp. Out of print.

This book of poems primarily about nature and women includes an autobiographical sketch.

RIDGE, MAJOR; WATIE, STAND; and
BOUDINOT, ELIAS, Cherokee
Cherokee Cavaliers: Forty Years of Cherokee History as Told in the Correspondence of the Ridge-Watie-Boudinot Families, ed. by Edward Everett Dale and Gaston Litton. Norman, Oklahoma: Univ. of Oklahoma Press, 1939. 319 pp. Illus. Out of print.

The letters of Ridge, Boudinot, Watie and their descendants, a group of Cherokees favoring removal from Georgia to Oklahoma, illustrate the violent controversy over the question of removal. Tribal internal strife during the 1850's and the effects of the War Between the States on the Cherokees are also discussed.

ROGERS, JOHN (CHIEF SNOW CLOUD), Chippewa
Red World and White: Memories of a Chippewa Boyhood. Norman, Oklahoma: Univ. of Oklahoma Press, 1974. 150 pp. $4.95.

Gathering from his memories his experiences as a boy on the reservation, the author reveals the life and customs of both the Chippewas and the whites. This book, first published in 1957, imparts information on the impact of the white society on reservation life.

ROMER, HERMAN, Eskimo, see BARR, MARTHA.

ROSS, JOHN, Cherokee
Letter from John Ross, Principal Chief of the Cherokee Nation of Indians. Washington: 1836. 31 pp. Out of print.

In answer to inquiries from a friend regarding Cherokee affairs with the U.S., Ross explains his objections to the 1835 treaty made between the Cherokees and the United States causing the removal of his tribe from Georgia. He also answers charges against him that he has no right to interfere in Cherokee affairs. Included is a copy of the 1836 protest of the Cherokee delegation against removal.

Message of the Principal Chief of the Cherokee Nation. Washington: Lester Hargrett, 1943. 11 pp. Out of print.

In this statement, originally published in 1864, Ross explains why the Cherokee Nation supports the Confederate States in the War Between the States. Also included is a *Declaration of the Cherokee People* which discusses the causes which led the Cherokees to unite with the Confederate States of America. The message is also reprinted in *Reply of the Southern Cherokees to the Memorial of Certain Delegates from the Cherokee Nation.* Washington: McGill and Witherow, 1866.

RUSSELL, NORMAN H., Cherokee
Indian Thoughts: The Small Songs of God. LaCrosse, Wisconsin: Juniper Press, 1972. 43 pp. $2.50 paperbound. Available from Juniper Press, 1310 Shorewood Drive, LaCrosse, Wisconsin 54601.

These 34 poems by Mr. Russell, a teacher of botany, reflect his interest in the natural environment.

SAINTE-MARIE, BUFFY, Cree
The Buffy Sainte-Marie Songbook. New York: Grosset and Dunlap, Inc., 1971. 224 pp. Illus. by author. $4.95 paperbound.

This book features 60 guitar arrangements of Buffy Sainte-Marie's songs with piano music for ten of her most popular songs. The songs deal with civil rights, Indian rights, women's rights, and love. There is a brief autobiographical introduction by Buffy Sainte-Marie.

SANCHEZ, WALTER, Zuni Pueblo, see
PEYNETSA, ANDREW.

SANDERS, THOMAS (NIPPAWANOCK), Cherokee,
and **PEEK, WILLIAM (METACOMET)**, Narragansett-Wampanoag, eds.
The Literature of the American Indian. Beverly Hills, California: Glencoe Press, 1973. 534 pp. $10.95.

Sanders and Peek present an anthology in textbook format containing Native American creation accounts, folktales, pre-Columbian poetry, oratory, selections from autobiographies, and biographies, selections on Native American religious and current poetry, prose and protest.

SANDO, JOE S., Jemez Pueblo
The Pueblo Indians. San Francisco: The Indian Historian Press, 1974. Illus. $9.00. Also paperbound: $6.00.

The author presents a two-part history of the Pueblo Indians. The first part contains historical data and descriptions of historical events together with biographies of many Pueblo people. The second part contains a fictionalized story of one Pueblo family as they lived in the past and as they dealt with their problems both before and after the Spanish Conquest.

SATTERLEE, CAPTAIN JOHN VALENTINE,
Menominee
Folklore of the Menomini Indians, with Alanson Skinner. Anthropological Papers of the American Museum of Natural History, Vol. 13, Part 3. New York: Published by the Trustees, 1915. pp. 217-546. Out of print.

The folklore of the Menominees, a tribe located in Wisconsin, includes sacred myths, trickster myths, fairy tales, "true" stories, and stories showing European influence.

SATTERLEE, CAPTAIN JOHN VALENTINE;
SATTERLEE, JOSEPH; SATTERLEE, JOSEPHINE,
et al., Menominee

Menomini Tales, ed. by Leonard Bloomfield. Publications of the American Ethnological Society, Vol. XII. New York: G. E. Stechert and Co., 1928. 608 pp. Out of print.

Texts in Menominee and English are arranged into pieces dealing with everyday life, past and present, songs, sermons, prayers and mystic narratives. Informants are cited for every text.

SATTERLEE, JOSEPH, Menominee, see
SATTERLEE, CAPTAIN JOHN VALENTINE.

SATTERLEE, JOSEPHINE, Menominee, see
SATTERLEE, CAPTAIN JOHN VALENTINE.

SAUBEL, KATHERINE SIVA, Cahuilla
Temalpakh (From the Earth: Cahuilla Indian Knowledge and Usage of Plants), with Lowell John Bean. Banning, California: Malki Museum Press, 1972. 225 pp. Illus. $10.00. Also paperbound: $6.50.

This book contains an ethnobotany of the Cahuilla Indians of southern California which encompasses the knowledge about and usage of more than 250 native plants. Information is included on Cahuilla plant lore and plant uses for medicine, food, and manufacture. Supplementary material in the book examines the controversial issue of aboriginal agriculture in southern California. Illustrated with photographs.

SEKAQUAPTEWA, EMORY, Hopi
"Preserving the Good Things of Hopi Life," in *Plural Society in the Southwest,* ed. by Edward H. Spicer and Raymond H. Thompson. New York: Interbook, Inc., 1972. pp. 239-260. $5.95.

The author discusses some history, events, and attitudes that demonstrate the nature of the dichotomy between the formalized governmental structure of the Hopi Tribal Council and the indigenous structure made up of tradition, custom, and religious influences.

SEKAQUAPTEWA, HELEN, Hopi
Me and Mine: The Life Story of Helen Sekaquaptewa, as told to Louise Udall. Tucson: Univ. of Arizona Press, 1969. 262 pp. $3.95 paperbound.

This autobiographical narrative describes the way a Hopi woman has been able to build a rewarding life by combining the best that the white and Hopi worlds have to offer.

SENUNGETUK, JOSEPH, Eskimo

Give or Take a Century: The Story of an Eskimo Family. San Francisco: The Indian Historian Press, 1970. 120 pp. Illus. by author. $12.95.

The author tells the history of an Eskimo family in Alaska as they move from a century filled with the customs, traditions, and life-ways of an ancient time into a new century in which they are confronted and confused by the mores, social life, and technology of a different culture.

SEWID, JAMES, Kwakiutl

Guests Never Leave Hungry: The Autobiography of James Sewid., a Kwakiutl Indian, ed. by James P. Spradley. New Haven: Yale Univ. Press, 1969. 310 pp. $10.00.

Sewid, an hereditary chief, tells the story of his life and the organizational and civic concerns of a growing Kwakiutl settlement in the Northwest.

SHAW, ANNA MOORE, Pima

Pima Indian Legends. Tucson: Univ. of Arizona Press, 1968. 111 pp. $2.50 paperbound.

Mrs. Shaw relates stories heard from her parents and grandparents and combines ancient Pima history with more current happenings.

SHISHMAREF DAY SCHOOL STUDENTS, Eskimo

Eskimo Cook Book, Anchorage, Alaska: Easter Seal Society for Alaska Crippled Children and Adults, 1952. $.50, $.60 postpaid (paperbound). Available from: Easter Seal Society for Alaska Crippled Children and Adults, P.O. Box 2432, Anchorage, Alaska 99510.

The students at Shishmaref Day School in Shishmaref, Alaska, supplied these recipes. Included are dishes such as salted duck, bear paws, salmon berries, walrus stew and Eskimo ice cream. This booklet presents a child's eye view of cooking. Some of the recipes include a description of how to obtain the food and prepare it. The cooking instructions often consist of "Put them in a pot to boil. Add salt and water."

SIMPSON, LOUIS; SIMPSON, TOM; McGUFF, PETE, *et al.,* Wishram

Wishram Texts, ed. by Edward Sapir. Publications of the American Ethnological Society, Vol. II. Leyden, Holland: E. J. Brill, 1909. pp. 1-235. Out of print.

The Wishram texts obtained on the Yakima Reservation in Washington in 1905, dictated by Simpson and others, are arranged into myths, customs, letters, non-mythological narratives, and an appendix containing supplementary upper Chinookian texts. Wishram and English texts.

SIMPSON, TOM, Wishram, see SIMPSON, LOUIS.

SINGER MAN, Navajo

"The Myth of Beautyway," ed. by Leland C. Wyman in *Beautyway: Navajo Ceremonial.* New York: Bollinger Foundation, Inc., 1957. pp. 41-125. Illus. Out of print.

This book contains the myth dictated by Singer Man of Arizona in 1932 to Father Bernard Haile, a Franciscan missionary who served actively among Indians for 54 years. Included is an introduction by Wyman about the Navajo Beautyway Ceremonial, its uses, mythology, songs, and geographical setting. A variant myth is also included. Singer Man's myth as it was recorded in Navajo is reproduced in a supplementary pamphlet correlated with the pages in the hardbound volume.

SITTING BULL, Sioux

Three Pictographic Autobiographies of Sitting Bull, ed. by M. W. Stirling. Smithsonian Miscellaneous Collections Vol. 97, No. 5. Washington: Smithsonian Institution, 1938. 57 pp. Out of print.

Three pictorial records made by Sitting Bull, a Sioux, represent feats which entitled him to special standing among his people. The three records known as the Kimball, Smith and Pettinger Pictographic Records contain respectively 54, 22, and 13 drawings. Interpretations accompany all the drawings which cover the period prior to the Battle of the Little Big Horn.

SNEVE, VIRGINIA DRIVING HAWK, Sioux

The Dakotas' Heritage. Sioux Falls, South Dakota: Brevet Press, 1973. 60 pp. $2.40. Available from: Brevet Press, 410 Northwestern Bank Building, Sioux Falls, South Dakota 57102.

This compilation of Indian place-names in South Dakota also includes historical and cultural information about Dakota Indians.

SON OF FORMER MANY BEADS, Navajo

The Ramah Navajos, ed. by Robert W. Young and William Morgan. Lawrence, Kansas: Bureau of Indian Affairs, 1967. 17 pp. $.10 paperbound. Available from Publications Service, Haskell Institute, Lawrence, Kansas 66044.

This booklet is one of a series of bilingual brochures. It deals with matters of historical significance to the Navajo, and discusses the development of the land problems of the Navajo in the Ramah (New Mexico) area.

STALKER, MARIE, Eskimo, see BARR, MARTHA.

STANDING BEAR, LUTHER, Sioux

Land of the Spotted Eagle. Boston: Houghton Mifflin Co., 1933. 259 pp. Out of print.

Chief Standing Bear describes his early life and the manners, customs, morals and characteristics of his people.

My Indian Boyhood. Boston: Houghton Mifflin Co., 1928. 288 pp. Illus. Out of print.

A Sioux chief, who was a member of the first class at Carlisle, tells of his home, school and reservation life, his marriage and work for the advancement of the Tribe.

My People, the Sioux, ed. by E. A. Brininstool. Boston: Houghton Mifflin Co., 1931. 189 pp. Illus. Out of print.

Chief Standing Bear relates memories of his boyhood, giving a great deal of information about the Sioux tribe and how their chiefs attain status.

STANDS IN TIMBER, JOHN, Cheyenne

Cheyenne Memories, A Folk History, with Margot Liberty and Robert M. Utley. New Haven: Yale Univ. Press, 1967. 330 pp. Illus. $10.00. Also paperbound: Lincoln: Univ. of Nebraska Press. $2.25.

Stands In Timber narrates a wide range of Cheyenne experience, from legendary times to life on the Northern Cheyenne Reservation in Montana. *Cheyenne Memories* represents his personal effort to preserve the history of his people.

STEWART, JACK, Paiute, see NEWLAND, SAM.

STEVENS, TOM; McGREGOR, WALTER; ISAAC,
et al., Haida
Haida Texts and Myths, recorded by John Reed Swanton. New York: Johnson Reprint Corp., 448 pp. Illus. $18.00.

Texts and myths obtained in British Columbia in 1900-01 are given in both Haida and English. Informants are cited for each story. Reprint of the U. S. Bureau of American Ethnology, Bulletin 29, 1905.

STIGGINS, GEORGE, Natchez
"A Historical Narration of the Genealogy, Tradition, and Downfall of the Ispocaga, or Creek Tribe of Indians, Written by One of the Tribe," Reprinted in 3 parts in the Appendix of Theron A. Nunez, Jr., "Creek Nativism and the Creek War of 1813-1814," *Ethnohistory* Vol. 5, No. 1, Winter, 1958. pp. 17-41, 131-175, 292-301. Out of print.

Written in the 1830's, Stiggins' account of the history and culture of the Creek Tribe of Alabama and Georgia is a rare source document about Indian life in the South and Indian-white conflicts.

STRONG, NATHANIEL, Seneca
Appeal to the Christian Community on the Condition and Prospects of the New York Indians. New York: E. B. Clayton, Printers, 1841. 65 pp. Out of print.

Strong refutes the basic points made in a book, written by the Society of Friends, which he says purports to misrepresent and undermine the ratification of a treaty concluded between the United States and the Seneca Tribe, located in New York. Strong tries to prove the treaty would be beneficial to the tribe.

STUMP, SARAIN, Shoshone
There Is My People Sleeping, Sidney, British Columbia: Gray's Publishing, Ltd., 1970. Unpaged. Illus. by author. $9.50.

A brief autobiography accompanies the drawings and poetry by Stump, a 28-year-old Shoshone from Wyoming.

SWEEZY, CARL, Arapaho
The Arapaho Way: A Memoir of an Indian Boyhood, as told to Althea Bass. New York: Clarkson N. Potter, Inc., 1966. 88 pp. Illus. by author. $5.00.

Mr. Sweezy, born in 1881, relates his memories of Arapaho culture's "old ways." His illustrations depict dances, hunts, games, dress, and ceremonies.

SWIMMER, Cherokee

The Swimmer Manuscript: Cherokee Sacred Formulas and Medicinal Prescriptions, ed. by James Mooney and Frans. M. Olbrechts. U. S. Bureau of American Ethnology, Bulletin 99. Washington: Government Printing Office, 1932. 309 pp. Illus. Out of print.

Ninety-six medicinal formulas and prescriptions in Cherokee and translated texts (originally written down in an unpaged blank book by Swimmer) are reproduced with a long introductory section surveying Cherokee medical lore and custom.

SWIMMER; AX, JOHN; WAFFORD, JAMES D., *et al.,* Cherokee

Myths of the Cherokees, ed. by James Mooney. Nashville, Tennessee: Charles Elder-Bookseller Publisher. 576 pp. $15.00. Available from: Charles Elder, 2115 Elliston Place, Nashville, Tennessee 37203.

Several Cherokee informants furnish a collection of Cherokee mythology including sacred myths, animal stories, local legends and historical traditions. A section of notes and a glossary are included. A long historical sketch of the Cherokees precedes the myths. This is a reprint of an extract from U. S. Bureau of American Ethnology, Nineteenth Annual Report, 1902.

SWIMMER; GAHUNI; INÂ´LI, *et al.,* Cherokee

"Sacred Formulas of the Cherokees," ed. by James Mooney, in *Myths of the Cherokee and Sacred Formulas of the Cherokee.* Nashville, Tennessee: Charles Elder-Bookseller, Publisher. pp. 307-397. $15.00. Available from: Charles Elder, 2115 Elliston Place, Nashville, Tennessee 37203.

These magic formulas, taken from their original Cherokee manuscripts, provide insights into the ancient religion of the Tribe and into the daily life and thought of the people.

TALAYESVA, DON C., Hopi

Sun Chief: The Autobiography of a Hopi Indian, ed. by Leo W. Simmons. New Haven: Yale Univ. Press, 1942. 460 pp. $12.50. Also paperbound: $3.95.

This frank autobiography describes Talayesva's first ten years (1890-1900) in the Hopi village of Oraibi, Arizona, and the subsequent decade spent in schools in Arizona and California.

TALL BULL, HENRY, Cheyenne

Cheyenne Fire Fighters. Billings, Montana: Montana Indian Publications, 1971. 39 pp. Illus. $1.00 paperbound.

This is about a crew of Cheyenne men who fight forest fires. The story opens with the sighting of smoke on the horizon by a forest ranger, describes how forest fires behave and details modern methods used to contain and control forest fires.

TAOS PUEBLO DAY SCHOOL STUDENTS, Taos Pueblo

Oo-Oonah Art: Taos Indian for 'Child', ed. by Constantine Aiello. Taos, New Mexico: Taos Pueblo Governor's Office, 1970. 52 pp. Illus. by students. $10.00. Available from: Taos Indian Children's Art Book, Box 239, Taos, New Mexico 87571.

A special collector's edition of 57 paintings and pencil drawings and poetry by children, 13 and 14 years old, in the seventh and eighth grades of the day-school of Taos Pueblo, New Mexico, 1967-68.

TATE, HENRY W., Tsimshian

Tsimshian Mythology, translated by Franz Boas. New York: Johnson Reprint Corp., pp. 58-392. $35.00.

This collection of 64 myths reflects the important traditions of the Tsimshian people (British Columbia). Reprint of U. S. Bureau of American Ethnology, Thirty-First Annual Report, 1916. For more Tsimshian texts, see *Tsimshian Texts,* U. S. Bureau of American Ethnology, Bulletin 27.

TATSEY, JOHN, Blackfeet

The Black Moccasin: Life on the Blackfeet Indian Reservation. Spokane, Washington: Curtis Art Gallery, 1971. 79 pp. Illus. $3.50 paperbound. Available from: Curtis Art Gallery, Davenport Hotel, 807 W. Sprague, Spokane, Washington 99210.

A collection of Tatsey's weekly columns for the *Glacier Reporter* of Browning, Montana, during the late 1950's and early 1960's. Tatsey, born in 1894, writes about many aspects of contemporary tribal life, including insights gained from his 18 years as a Blackfeet tribal policeman. Also included is a verbatim transcription of tape recordings made by Tatsey in which he interprets Blackfeet names, legends, and tribal ceremonies. The illustrations are by Albert Racine, also Blackfeet.

TCHIKILLI, Creek

A Migration Legend of the Creek Indians, ed. by Albert S. Gatschet. New York: Kraus Reprint Co., 458 pp. (2 vols. in one). $17.50.

Tchikilli's Kasi'hta legend is presented in the Creek and Hitchiti languages as well as English, with critical commentary and full glossaries to all texts. It was delivered by Tchikilli, head chief of the Upper and Lower Creeks, to Governor Oglethorpe of Georgia. This is a reprint of a book published in 1888 by Daniel Brinton as Volume 4 in his Library of Aboriginal American Literature.

TETSO, JOHN, Slavey

Trapping Is My Life. Toronto: Peter Martin Associates, Ltd., 1970. 116 pp. Illus. $4.95.

This series of short stories by a Canadian Indian trapper who lived and worked near Fort Simpson, Northwest Territory, contains contemporary information about trapping, moose, beaver, rabbit hunting, fishing, summer and winter camps and his family. Also included is a section of letters exchanged between the Tetsos and the Molsons of Montreal who befriended the Tetsos in 1962.

THOMAS, ROBERT K., Cherokee

"The Role of the Church in Indian Adjustment," in *For Every North American Indian Who Begins to Disappear, I Also Begin to Disappear.* Toronto: Neewin Publishing Co., Ltd., 1971. pp. 87-106. $3.75 paperbound.

The author briefly characterizes the general nature of American Indian societies, suggests the external conditions preventing normal social and cultural adjustment, and recommends a new role for churches that will enable Indians to adjust culturally.

"Survey Report to the Anglican Church on the Northwest Territories," and John A. MacKenzie, in *For Every North American Indian Who Begins to Disappear, I Also Begin to Disappear.* Toronto: Neewin Publishing Co., Ltd., 1971. pp. 109-139. $3.75 paperbound.

This is a report on the contemporary social and economic conditions of Canadian Indians and Eskimos in the MacKenzie River, Inuvik, and Yellowknife—Fort Rae areas. The authors make recommendations to the Canadian Anglican and Catholic churches to improve the life of the Natives in these regions.

THOMPSON, CHIEF ALBERT EDWARD, Chippewa

Chief Peguis and His Descendants. Winnipeg, Manitoba: Peguis Publishers, 1973. 86 pp. Illus. $6.00.

The author, born in 1900, tells the story of Chief Peguis, his great great grandfather, who leads a band of Chippewas from Sault Ste. Marie, Ontario to the Red River country in the 1790's. Chief Peguis' encounters with other Indian tribes and whites are described. The story of the Chief's descendants and their life on the Peguis Reserve as well as an autobiography are included.

THOMPSON, JEAN; MITCHELL, WAYNE; NEPTUNE, MARTIN, *et al.,* Penobscot
"Voices-1, 2, 3" in *Glooskap's Children: Encounters with the Penobscot Indians of Maine,* by Peter Anastas. Boston: Beacon Press, 1973. pp. 52-81, 115-133, 159-168. Illus. $6.95.

In a series of tape recorded interviews, Jean Thompson and four other Penobscot Indians describe what it feels like to be an Indian living on a reservation in Maine in the midst of a dominant white culture in the 1970's. Also included is a collection of Penobscot myths and folktales found in out-of-print sources.

TILLOHASH, TONY, Paiute, and
MACK, CHARLIE, Ute
Texts of the Kaibah Paiutes and Uintah Utes, ed. by Edward Sapir. Proceedings of the American Academy of Arts and Sciences Vol. 65, No. 2, September, 1930. pp. 297-535. Out of print.

Collected by Sapir in the Southwest in 1909-1910, these texts include a set of Paiute myths and non-mythical texts and Ute myths. Notes for both the Paiute and Ute texts and the English translations of both are included.

TOM; GEORGE, HAMILTON; WILLIAMS, FRANK, *et al.,* Nootka
Nootka Texts. Collected by Edward Sapir and Morris Swadesh. Philadelphia: Linguistic Society of America, 1939. pp. 1-234. Out of print.

These 44 texts of folktales and ethnological narratives of the Nootka, a people located on Vancouver Island, are presented in the original and in English translation.

TOWENDOLLY, GRANT, Wintu
A Bag of Bones, ed. by Marcelle Masson. Healdsburg, California: Naturegraph Publishers, 1966. 130 pp. $5.50. Also paperbound: $2.50.

Stories and legends of the Wintu Indians of northern California are told by a member of the tribe.

TRAVELLER BIRD (TSISGHWANAI), Cherokee
Tell Them They Lie: The Sequoyah Myth. Los Angeles: Westernlore Publishers, 1971. 150 pp. Illus. $7.95.

The author presents a controversial theory regarding Sequoyah and the Cherokee syllabary. Traveller Bird maintains the symbols in the syllabary were not devised by Sequoyah but were brought to the Cherokees by the Taliwas (people from the plateau country of the Great Plains) on gold tablets long before the coming of the Europeans.

The Path to Snowbird Mountain: Cherokee Legends.
New York: Farrar, Straus, and Giroux, Inc., 1972. 96 pp. Illus. $3.95.

Sixteen stories of animals and men, hunters, and creation of the world and the beginnings of fire are retold.

TUBBEE, OKAH, Choctaw
Sketch of the Life of Okah Tubbee, Alias William Chubbee. Springfield, Massachusetts: H. S. Taylor, 1848. 84 pp. Out of print.

Okah Tubbee tells of his life as an American Indian slave. Taken from his Choctaw family as a young boy and placed by a white master in the home of a black slave woman, Tubbee relates his childhood experiences in Natchez, Mississippi and his subsequent life in the south in the first half of the 19th century. He also tells the story of his first encounter with Indians in Mississippi and the rediscovery of his Indian heritage. Also included is a brief autobiography by Tubbee's wife.

TWO LEGGINGS, Crow
Two Leggings: The Making of a Crow Warrior, ed. by Peter Nabokov. New York: Thomas Y. Crowell Co., 1967. 226 pp. $2.95 paperbound.

This first-person account of the everyday life of a nineteenth-century Crow Indian man provides a primary source for understanding, and witnessing in action, the religious and social values of a Plains Indian people.

VALOR, PALMER, Apache, see PRINCE, ANNA.

VARGAS, ROSENDO, Picuris Pueblo
Picuris Children's Stories with Texts and Songs, ed. by J. P. Harrington and Helen H. Roberts, U. S. Bureau of American Ethnology, Forty-third Annual Report. Washington: Government Printing Office, 1928. pp. 289-447. Out of print.

These children's stories, songs, folkways were dictated by Vargas just as he heard them told by his grandfather in northern New Mexico. Picuris and English texts.

VAUDRIN, BILL, Chippewa
Tanaina Tales from Alaska. Norman: Univ. of Oklahoma Press, 1969. 132 pp. $4.95.

The author, who has lived and taught in Alaska for years, has gathered a collection of stories handed down through the generations.

VELARDE, PABLITA, Santa Clara Pueblo
Old Father, the Story Teller. Tucson, Arizona: Dale Stuart King, 1960. 66 pp. Illus. by author. Out of print.

An Indian painter writes the stories and legends she heard from her grandfather and great-grandfather in the Southwest.

VILLASENOR, DAVID, Otomi
Tapestries in Sand: The Spirit of Indian Sandpainting. Healdsburg, California: Naturegraph Publishers, 1966. 112 pp. Illus. $6.25. Also paperbound: $3.25.

The author, who has learned sandpainting from Navajo medicine men, writes about this ancient art and its meanings.

VIZENOR, GERALD, Chippewa
anishinabe adisokan: Tales of the People. Minneapolis: The Nodin Press, 1970. 150 pp. Illus. $2.45 paperbound.

This collection of tales printed almost a century ago in *The Progress,* a weekly newspaper of the White Earth Reservation in Minnesota, is concerned with the origin and religion of the anishinabe (Chippewa) and the birth and life of Manabozho—the trickster. Illustrations are reproductions of original Chippewa pictomyths. Also included are a list of Chippewa words and cultural information about the tribe.

anishinabe nagamon: Songs of the People. Minneapolis: The Nodin Press, 1970. 134 pp. Illus. $1.95 paperbound.

This is a collection of songs and poems interpreted and re-expressed from original anishinabe song transcriptions by the author. Illustrations of pictomyths accompany the songs. A section of interpretative notes regarding the songs and pictomyths is included.

The Everlasting Sky: New Voices from the People Named the Chippewa. New York: Crowell-Collier Press, 1972. 140 pp. Illus. $4.95.

The author discusses the tribal past of the Chippewa (anishinabe) and the contemporary experiences of oshki anishinabe (the new people of the woodland) in Minnesota and Wisconsin. The oshki anishinabe convey material about their family, city and reservation life, law enforcement, and feelings about changes and preserving anishinabe heritage.

WAFFORD, JAMES D., see SWIMMER; AX, JOHN; WAFFORD, JAMES D., *et al.*, Cherokee

WAHNENAUHI (LUCY LOWRY HOYT KEYS), Cherokee
The Wahnenauhi Manuscript, ed. by Jack Frederick Kilpatrick. U. S. Bureau of American Ethnology Bulletin 196. Anthropological Papers, No. 77. Washington: Government Printing Office, 1966. pp. 175-213. Illus. Out of print.

This document, written about 1889, contains information on Cherokee history and ethnology and material about Sequoyah and other Cherokee figures, from the point of view of an acculturated Cherokee.

WARREN, WILLIAM WHIPPLE, Chippewa
History of the Ojibway Nation. Minneapolis: Ross and Haines, 1957. 527 pp. $10.00.

This classic history of the Chippewas (Ojibways), first published in 1885 and based on the work of tribal historians and some eye-witnesses, covers five centuries up to the mid-nineteenth century. Nearly half of the book is devoted to the late eighteenth and early nineteenth centuries. The author describes customs of the tribe at that time. Attitudes reflect the late nineteenth century and should be considered in this light. This is a reprint of *History of the Ojibways Based upon Traditions and Oral Statements.*

WATCHES-ALL, Gros Ventre, see JONES, BILL.

WATIE, STAND, Cherokee, see RIDGE, MAJOR.

WAUBAGESHIG (HARVEY McCUE), Chippewa, ed.
The Only Good Indian: Essays by Canadian Indians. Toronto: New Press, 1970. 188 pp. $8.50. Also paperbound: $3.50.

Canadian Indians in a collection of 13 documents (poetry, a play, essays, "Red Paper") discuss and condemn contemporary Canadian Indian affairs policy.

WEBB, GEORGE, Pima

A Pima Remembers. Tucson: Univ. of Arizona Press, 1959. 126 pp. Illus. $2.95.

Mr. Webb relates Pima history and traditions in the form of short stories. The book is designed both to acquaint young Pima readers who live in the Southwest with their own traditions and to familiarize white readers with the position of Pimas in modern American life.

WELCH, JAMES, Blackfeet

Riding the Earthboy 40: Poems by James Welch. New York: World Publishing Co., 1971. 54 pp. Out of print.

The poetry by Mr. Welch, who helped his family tenant farm forty acres belonging to Earthboy, describes his growing up, his days spent with the Blackfeet Tribe of Montana, and working close to nature, as well as the days filled with prejudice and exploitation.

WHITE BULL, JOSEPH, Sioux

The Warrior Who Killed Custer: The Personal Narrative of Chief Joseph White Bull, trans. and ed. by James H. Howard. Lincoln: Univ. of Nebraska Press, 1969. 84 pp. Illus. by author. $6.95.

Writing in Dakota (Sioux) and using traditional pictographs, Chief White Bull describes hunts and battles in which he participated, including three accounts of the killing of Custer. Also included is a traditional winter count of the western Sioux, covering the years from 1764 to 1931.

WHITEWOLF, JIM, Kiowa-Apache

Jim Whitewolf: The Life of a Kiowa Apache Indian, ed. by Charles S. Brant. New York: Dover Books, 1969. 144 pp. $1.75 paperbound.

This life story of a Kiowa-Apache man born in the second half of the nineteenth century in Oklahoma, was dictated in 1949 and 1950 and describes tribal society under white influence.

WILLIAMS, FRANK, Nootka, see TOM.

WILLOYA, WILLIAM, Eskimo

Warriors of the Rainbow, co-authored by Vinson Brown. Healdsburg, California: Naturegraph Publishers, 1962. 104 pp. Illus. $5.50. Also paperbound: $2.50.

A study of Indian dreams is accompanied by full-color reproductions of paintings done by Indian artists. An appendix gives the scientific basis for the study.

WINNIE, LUCILLE "JERRY," (SAH-GAN-DE-OH), Seneca-Cayuga

Sah-gan-de-oh, the Chief's Daughter. New York: Vantage Press, 1968. 190 pp. Out of print.

This is an autobiography of a twentieth century Seneca-Cayuga woman who grew up on reservations in Oklahoma, Montana, and Kansas.

WOLF KILLER, Omaha(?)

Ploughed Under: The Story of an Indian Chief Told by Himself, ed. by William J. Harsha (?). New York: ?, 1881. 268 pp. Out of print.

The author narrates a life of suffering in the nineteenth century: warfare with other tribes, subjugation to Indian agents, etc. The book illustrates the author's belief that, while the "ploughshare" benefits vegetable life, Indian bodies and souls go under the advancing "ploughshare" of American civilization on the western Plains. The book may be read as a plea for respect of Indian cultures.

WOODEN LEG, Cheyenne

Wooden Leg: A Warrior Who Fought Custer, as told to Thomas B. Marquis. Lincoln: Univ. of Nebraska Press, 1962. 389 pp. $2.25 paperbound.

This reprint of a 1931 edition is the narrative of a Cheyenne warrior who fought against Custer at the Battle of the Little Big Horn. It includes observations on Cheyenne daily life and tribal customs from the mid-1850's to the 1920's.

WUTTUNEE, WILLIAM I. C., Cree

Ruffled Feathers: Indians in Canadian Society. Calgary, Alberta, Canada: Bell Books, Ltd., 1971. 174 pp. $5.50. Also paperbound: $2.50.

Wuttunee, a Cree born in Saskatchewan, presents a book of controversial opinions. Because he believes "segregation and progress are not compatible in the case of the Indian," he criticizes the reservation system, outmoded treaties, and Red Power advocates and suggests integration, involvement, education, and hard work are the keys to Indian survival and progress.

WYNECOOP, DAVID C., Spokane

Children of the Sun: A History of the Spokane Indians. Wellpinit, Washington: Published by the Author, 1969. 80 pp. Illus. $2.75 paperbound. Available from: Spokane Tribe, P. O. Box 86, Wellpinit, Washington 99040.

The author covers the history of his tribe located in Washington before and after the arrival of Europeans until the present day. The book contains a bibliography and several appendixes of historical government documents pertaining to Spokane land, Spokane-English dictionaries, myths, and newspaper articles about the tribe.

YAZZIE, ETHELON, Navajo

Navajo History, Volume I. Chinle, Arizona: Navajo Community College Press, 1971. 100 pp. Illus. $12.00. Also paperbound: $6.00. Available from: Navajo Curriculum Center, Rough Rock Demonstration School, Chinle, Arizona 86503.

Volume I includes accounts of the various underworlds, the emergence from them by the Navajo people, the origin of Navajo clans—all told from the Navajo point of view. Stories of Navajo elders and medicine men were recorded in countless sessions of interviewing. Skilled Navajo transcribers researched and refined the stories which were then translated into English. Additional volumes of *Navajo History* are expected to follow. The entire series is to be available in both Navajo and English.

WORKING INDIANS CIVIL ASSOCIATION,
Dakota Sioux

A Dakota-English Dictionary. Pierre, South Dakota: Working Indians Civil Association, 1969. Pages unreported. $6.00. Available from: W.I.C.A., Box 537, Pierre, South Dakota 57501.

The purpose of this book is to impart an appreciation of Siouan heritage and culture through a study of Dakota.

WRIGHT, MURIEL HAZEL, Choctaw

"American Indian Corn Dishes," *Chronicles of Oklahoma,* Vol. 36, No. 2. Oklahoma City: Oklahoma Historical Society, 1958. pp. 155-166. Out of print.

This article presents the tribal names, preparation, uses, and dishes made from corn by the "Five Civilized Tribes" (*i.e.,* Chickasaw, Chocktaw, Cherokee, Creek, and Seminole).

A Guide to the Indian Tribes of Oklahoma. Norman: Univ. of Oklahoma Press, 1965. 300 pp. Illus. $6.95.

Brief histories of sixty-five tribes either indigenous to Oklahoma or relocated there by the federal government are augmented by a summary of the role played by Indians in the evolution of the Oklahoma area.

Oklahoma: A History of the State and Its People, with Joseph B. Thoburn. New York: Lewis Historical Publishing Co., Inc., 1929. 4 vols. Out of print.

Volumes I and II of this work cover Oklahoma history from ancient times to the 1920's. Volumes III and IV contain the biographies of prominent Oklahomans.

Springplace: Moravian Mission and the Ward Family of the Cherokee Nation. Guthrie, Oklahoma: Cooperative Publishing Co., 1940. 93 pp. Illus. Out of print.

This volume presents a brief outline of the development of the Cherokee Nation and traces the role of Christianity in Cherokee history.

YELLOW BROW; PLENTY-HAWK; YOUNG CRANE,
et al., Crow

Crow Texts, ed. by Robert H. Lowie. Berkeley: Univ. of California Press, 1960. 550 pp. Out of print.

Crow texts collected between 1906 and 1916 and in 1931 on the Crow Reservation in Montana give accounts of actual events, customs, myths, and tales. Historical and semi-historical information, songs, prayers and short stories are also included. The informants' names are cited by many of the texts. Crow and English texts.

YELLOW ROBE, ROSEBUD (LACOTAWIN), Sioux

An Album of the American Indian. New York: Franklin Watts, Inc., 1969. 96 pp. Illus. $4.95.

Paintings, drawings, and photographs, accompanied by a brief text, serve to illustrate various facets of American Indian cultures and history from past to present. Although designed primarily for young adults, this album will be of interest to all ages.

YELLOW WOLF, Nez Perce

Yellow Wolf: His Own Story, ed. by Lucullus Virgil McWhorter. Caldwell, Idaho: Caxton Printers, Ltd., 1940. 324 pp. Illus. Out of print.

This narrative by Yellow Wolf, recorded from 1908-1935, includes some information on his earlier life but in the main is Yellow Wolf's story of the Nez Perce War of 1877 from its inception to its ending. Several chapters on the aftermath of the war from Yellow Wolf's point of view are included.

YOUNG, LUCY, Wailaki
"Out of the Past: A True Indian Story," as told to Edith V. A. Murray in the *California Historical Society Quarterly,* Vol. XX, No. 4. Dec. 1941. pp. 349-364. Out of print.

These memoirs were dictated in 1939 by a ninety-year-old woman who recalled her childhood and the occurrences of everyday life in California. The major part of the narrative takes place in 1862.

YOUNG, TOM, Maidu
Maidu Texts, ed. by Roland B. Dixon. Publications of the American Ethnological Society, Vol. 4. Leyden, Holland: E. J. Brill, 1912. 241 pp. Out of print.

These eighteen myths, the most commonly told by this California tribe, include the creation myth and tales relating to coyote. Maidu texts and translations.

YOUNG BEAR, RAY, Sauk and Fox, see DELORIA, VINE V., Sr.

YOUNG CRANE, Crow, see YELLOW BROW.

YUINTH-ZEZI, Navajo
Myth of Sóntso Hatrál, recorded and retold in shorter form by Mary C. Wheelwright. Bulletin No. 2. Santa Fe, New Mexico: Museum of Navajo Ceremonial Art, Inc., 1957. pp. 1-9. Out of print.

This brief myth tells of Younger Brother, who is deceived by Coyote, and his adventures among the Black Star people.

ZITKALA-SA (GERTRUDE BONNIN), Sioux
American Indian Stories. Washington: Hayworth Publishing House, 1921. 195 pp. Out of print.

This collection of stories about the Sioux in the late nineteenth and early twentieth centuries, also contains memories of the author's childhood and an explanation of why the author prefers Indian religion.

Oklahoma's Poor Rich Indians: An Orgy of Graft and Exploitation of the Five Civilized Tribes—Legalized Robbery, with Charles H. Fabens and Matthew K. Sniffen. Publication of the Indian Rights Association, Second Series, No. 127. Philadelphia: Indian Rights Association, 1924. 39 pp. Out of print.

This is the report of an investigation in eastern Oklahoma in 1923 which describes how the property of members of the Five Civilized Tribes is being stolen because Congress passed an act taking from the Interior Department all jurisdiction over Indian probate and transferring it to local county courts.

Old Indian Legends. Boston: Ginn and Co., 1901.
165 pp. Illus. Out of print.

These 14 tales from the Dakotas retell the adventures of Iktomi, the snare weaver; the Eater, and Old Double-Face.

ZO-TOM, Kiowa, see HOWLING WOLF.

ZUNI, FLORA; ZUNI, LINDA; CLARENCE,
et al., Zuni Pueblo
Zuni Mythology, ed. by Ruth Benedict. New York:
AMS Press, Inc., 2 Vols. $47.50. Per vol.: $25.00.

In 1922-23, Flora Zuni and seven other members of the Pueblo recorded these tales of Kachinas, courtship, despised and unacknowledged children, husbands and wives, conflicts with witches, war and famine, and animals. An introductory essay analyzes the themes common to Zuni folklore. This is a reprint of Columbia Univ. Contributions to Anthropology Vol. 21, 1935.

Zuni Texts, ed. by Ruth Bunzel. Publications of the
American Ethnological Society, Vol. XV. New York:
G. E. Stechert and Co., 1933. 285 pp. Out of print.

Flora Zuni and seven other Zunis provide ethnological material and tales in Zuni texts (English translation provided). The autobiography of Linda Zuni, one of the informants, is included on pages 74-97.

ZUNI, LINDA, Zuni Pueblo, see ZUNI, FLORA.

ZUNI PUEBLO
The Zunis: Self-Portrayals, translated by Alvina Quam. Albuquerque: Univ. of New Mexico Press, 1972. 245 pp. Photographs of tribal elders. $7.95. $3.95 paperbound.

Here for the first time in print are forty-six stories from the great oral literature of the Zunis of New Mexico. The creation story, rituals of masked dances, farming and hunting practices, battles, fables and history are all recorded in this book. There are tales of ghosts and personified animals, as well as fables told to discipline children or to warn them against foolhardy bravery and braggadocio. Some of the stories are simply for entertainment and some deal with the problems of modern society.

List of Publishers

AMS Press, Inc.
56 East 13th Street
New York, N. Y. 10003

Harry N. Abrams, Inc.
110 East 59th Street
New York, N. Y. 10022

Alaska Methodist University Press
Wesley Drive
Anchorage, Alaska 99504

American Heritage Press
1221 Avenue of the Americas
New York, N. Y. 10020

Archon
Shoe String Press
995 Sherman Avenue
Hamden, Conn. 06514

Atheneum
122 East 42nd Street
New York, N. Y. 10017

Avon Books
959 Eighth Avenue
New York, N. Y. 10019

Ballantine Books, Inc.
101 Fifth Avenue
New York, N. Y. 10003

Beacon Press
25 Beacon Street
Boston, Mass. 02108

Bell Books Ltd.
206 Seventh Avenue, Southwest
Calgary, Alberta, Canada

Capricorn Books
200 Madison Avenue
New York, N. Y. 10016

Chalfant Press, Inc.
Bishop, Calif. 93514

Clarke, Irwin & Co., Inc.
Clarwin House
791 St. Clair Avenue West
Toronto 10, Ontario, Canada

Thomas Y. Crowell Co.
201 Park Avenue South
New York, N. Y. 10003

Crowell-Collier Press
866 Third Avenue
New York, N. Y. 10022

Crown Publishers, Inc.
419 Park Avenue South
New York, N. Y. 10016

The John Day Co., Inc.
257 Park Avenue South
New York, N. Y. 10010

J. M. Dent & Sons (Canada), Ltd.
100 Scarsdale Road
Don Mills 404, Ontario, Canada

Dial Press
750 Third Avenue
New York, N. Y. 10017

Dillon Press
500 South Third Street
Minneapolis, Minn. 55415

Doubleday and Co., Inc.
Garden City, N. Y. 11530

Dover Publications, Inc.
180 Varick Street
New York, N. Y. 10014

H. P. Dutton & Co., Inc.
201 Park Avenue South
New York, N. Y. 10003

Farrar, Straus and Giroux, Inc.
19 Union Square West
New York, N. Y. 10003

Fawcett Publications, Inc.
Fawcett Place
Greenwich, Conn. 06830

Follett Publishing Co.
1010 West Washington Boulevard
Chicago, Ill. 60607

Ira J. Friedman, Inc.
Box 270
Port Washington, N. Y. 11050

Glencoe Press
8701 Wilshire Boulevard
Beverly Hills, Calif. 90211

Gray's Publishing, Ltd.
Box 2160
Sidney, British Columbia, Canada

Griffin House Publishers
455 King Street, West
Toronto, Ontario M5V 1K7
Canada

Grosset and Dunlap, Inc.
51 Madison Avenue
New York, N. Y. 10010

Harper & Row, Publishers
49 East 33rd Street
New York, N. Y. 10016

Holt, Rinehart & Winston, Inc.
383 Madison Avenue
New York, N. Y. 10017

Houghton Mifflin Co.
2 Park Street
Boston, Mass. 02107

Hurtig Publishers
10451 (rear) Jasper Avenue
Edmonton, Alberta T5J 1Z1
Canada

The Indian Historian Press
1451 Masonic Avenue
San Francisco, Calif. 94117

Indiana University Press
Tenth and Morton Streets
Bloomington, Ind. 47401

Interbook Incorporated
545 Eighth Avenue
New York, N. Y. 10018

Johnson Reprint Corp.
111 Fifth Avenue
New York, N. Y. 10003

Alfred A. Knopf, Inc.
201 East 50th Street
New York, N. Y. 10022

Kraus Reprint Co.
16 East 46th Street
New York, N. Y. 10017

Liveright
386 Park Avenue South
New York, N. Y. 10016

McClelland and Stewart, Ltd.
25 Hollinger Road
Toronto 16, Ontario, Canada

McGill-Queen's University Press
3458 Redpath Street
Montreal 109, P. Q., Canada

McGraw-Hill Book Co.
1221 Avenue of the Americas
New York, N. Y. 10020

McGraw-Hill Co. of Canada, Ltd.
330 Progress Avenue
Scarborough 707, Ontario, Canada

The Macmillan Company
866 Third Avenue
New York, N. Y. 10022

Malki Museum Press
11-795 Fields Road
Banning, Calif. 92220

Peter Martin Associates, Inc.
17 Inkerman Street
Toronto 5, Ontario, Canada

Edward A. Milligan
Bottineau
North Dakota 58318

Charles J. Musson, Ltd.
30 Lesmill Road
Don Mills, Ontario, Canada

Montana Indian Publications
Level 4
Stapleton Building
Billings, Mont. 59101

William Morrow & Co., Inc.
105 Madison Avenue
New York, N. Y. 10016

Museum of the American Indian
Broadway at 155th Street
New York, N. Y. 10032

Native American Publishing Co.
P. O. Box 2033
Santa Clara, Calif. 95051

Naturegraph Publishers
8339 West Dry Creek Road
Healdsburg, Calif. 95448

The Naylor Company
1015 Culebra Avenue
San Antonio, Texas 78201

Neewin Publishing Co., Ltd.
11½ Spadina Road
Toronto 179, Ontario, Canada

New American Library, Inc.
1301 Avenue of the Americas
New York, N. Y. 10019

New Press
553 Richmond Street West
Toronto, Ontario M52 1Y6
Canada

New York Graphic Society, Ltd.
140 Greenwich Avenue
Greenwich, Conn. 06830

The Nodin Press
519 North Third Street
Minneapolis, Minn. 55401

Northern Michigan University Press
Marquette, Mich. 49855

Northland Press
Box N
Flagstaff, Arizona 86001

Oxford University Press
200 Madison Avenue
New York, N. Y. 10016

Paperjacks
30 Lesmill Road
Don Mills, Ontario, Canada

Peguis Publishers
462 Hargrave Street
Winnipeg, Manitoba R3A 0X
Canada

Pocket Books
630 Fifth Avenue
New York, N. Y. 10020

Clarkson N. Potter, Inc.
419 Park Avenue South
New York, N. Y. 10016

Praeger Publishers, Inc.
111 Fourth Avenue
New York, N. Y. 10003

Prentice-Hall, Inc.
Englewood Cliffs, N. J. 07632

Ross and Haines
11 East Lake
Minneapolis, Minn. 55408

Scholarly Press, Inc.
22929 Industrial Drive East
St. Clair Shores, Mich. 48080

Simon and Schuster, Inc.
630 Fifth Avenue
New York, N. Y. 10020

Peter Smith
6 Lexington Avenue
Gloucester, Mass. 01930

Southern Methodist University Press
Dallas, Texas 75222

Southwest Museum
Highland Park
Los Angeles, Calif. 90042

Syracuse University Press
Box 8
University Station
Syracuse, N. Y. 13210

Teachers College Press
Columbia University
1234 Amsterdam Avenue
New York, N. Y. 10027

University of Arizona Press
Box 3398
Tucson, Arizona 85722

University of California Press
2223 Fulton Street
Berkeley, Calif. 94720

University of Chicago Press
5801 Ellis Avenue
Chicago, Ill. 60637

University of Michigan Press
Ann Arbor, Mich. 48106

University of Nebraska Press,
901 North 17th Street
Lincoln, Nebr. 68508

University of Nevada Press
Reno, Nevada 89107

University of New Mexico Press
Albuquerque, N. M. 87106

University of Oklahoma Press
1005 Asp Avenue
Norman, Okla. 73069

University of South Dakota Press
Vermillion, S. D. 57069

University of Washington Press
Seattle, Wash. 98195

University of Wisconsin Press
Box 1379
Madison, Wisc. 53071

Viking Press
625 Madison Avenue
New York, N. Y. 10022

Vintage Books
c/o Random House
201 East 50th Street
New York, N. Y. 10022

Franklin Watts, Inc.
845 Third Avenue
New York, N. Y. 10022

Westernlore Press
Box 41073
Eagle Rock Station
Los Angeles, Calif. 90041

Yale University Press
149 York Street
New Haven, Conn. 06511